John Lydgate

Twayne's English Authors Series

George D. Economou, Editor

University of Oklahoma

TEAS 407

John Lydgate leaving Canterbury with the pilgrims
from the Prologue to the *Siege of Thebes*
(British Library MS. Royal 18.D.ii)

(3rd from rt.?)

John Lydgate

By Lois A. Ebin

Barnard College

Twayne Publishers • Boston

John Lydgate

Lois A. Ebin

Published by Twayne Publishers
A Division of G. K. Hall & Company
70 Lincoln Street
Boston, Massachusetts 02111

Book Production by Elizabeth Todesco
Book Design by Barbara Anderson

Printed on permanent/durable acid-free
paper and bound in the United States of
America.

Library of Congress Cataloging in Publication Data

Ebin, Lois.
John Lydgate.

(Twayne's English authors series ; TEAS 407)
Bibliography: p. 155
Includes index.
1. Lydgate, John, 1370?–1451?—Criticism and
interpretation. I. Title. II. Series.
PR2037.E2 1985 821'.2 85–731
ISBN 0–8057–6898–X

Contents

About the Author

Lois A. Ebin received her Ph.D. from Columbia University. She has taught at Barnard College, New York University, and Smith College. Her previous publications include *Vernacular Poetics in the Middle Ages* and articles and reviews on medieval literature that have appeared in the *Chaucer Review*, *Philological Quarterly*, *Studies in Scottish Literature*, *Annuale Mediaevale*, and *Speculum*.

Preface

Judged by his contemporaries an equal and, in some cases, a superior poet to Chaucer, John Lydgate, Monk of Bury, occupies the position of the most influential writer between the flowering of Middle English literature in the age of Chaucer, Gower, Langland, and the *Gawain* poet in the fourteenth century and the beginning of the Renaissance in England in the sixteenth. In volume, his writing includes more than 145,000 lines, twice the corpus of Shakespeare and three times that of Chaucer. In range, it encompasses every important medieval genre, sacred and profane—epic, romance, allegory, fable, saints' life, satire, mumming, and lyric. Lydgate's efforts are supported by some of the most powerful patrons of the period, men like Humphrey, duke of Gloucester, the earls of Salisbury and Warwick, and kings Henry IV, Henry V, and Henry VI. For his peers and immediate successors, Lydgate's poetry is an important source of thematic and stylistic material, a quarry to mine in their own writing, and, for the best of these poets, a source of experimentation and innovation. In their imitations and tributes, they admire above all Lydgate's sententiousness and his eloquence, his importance as an official public and didactic poet, and his role in extending the limits of their literary English.[1]

But many of the same qualities that appealed to Lydgate's contemporaries are a source of concern for modern readers in dealing with his poems. We find it difficult to appreciate a poet who is prolix rather than brief, rhetorical and eloquent rather than allusive, and overtly didactic rather than subtle or ironic, a poet whose pen turns with similar ease to long epics on the fall of Troy and Thebes and a treatise for a laundress or a satire on women's dress. Consequently, in the nineteenth and twentieth centuries, Lydgate suffers the fate of a much maligned and underrated poet, one who is admired in small doses but neglected in bulk. For most readers, it is difficult to reconcile the contradiction between the medieval and modern responses.

In part, Lydgate has suffered from the critical approaches taken to his work. Most frequently, he is treated as a poor imitator of Chaucer and a questionable heir to the great poets of the fourteenth century. Saintsbury, for example, sums up this view in the *Cambridge History of English Literature,* suggesting that Lydgate, though an imitator of Chaucer, lacks "Chaucerian strength" of humor, "Chaucerian vigour, Chaucerian pathos, Chaucerian vividness of description."[2] More recently, critics have attempted to revive Lydgate's reputation by considering him as a transition poet who, though less interesting in his own right than the fourteenth-century poets, is crucial to an understanding of the Renaissance. Walter Schirmer first articulates this interpretation in an article and then a book entitled *John Lydgate: A Study of the Culture of the Fifteenth Century.* Studying each of Lydgate's poems in depth against a detailed historical background, he suggests that Lydgate concluded the Middle Ages in England and prepared the way for the Renaissance to begin.[3] Alain Renoir, in *The Poetry of John Lydgate,* argues this position even more emphatically than Schirmer, defining the Renaissance themes in Lydgate's work and concluding that Lydgate is a "poet in transition" and "can be done justice" only if we approach him from this point of view.[4] Finally, a third group of critics attempts to justify Lydgate's poetry on historical grounds either by defining, as H. S. Bennett and Eleanor Hammond do, the conditions peculiar to the period—the disintegration of medieval social ideals, the constant warfare at home and abroad, the "stereotyping society" of the aristocracy, the rise of a new bourgeois reading public, the invention and widespread use of printing—which produce a climate hostile to the development of great literature, or by attempting, as Derek Pearsall does, to make his poetry more accessible to the modern reader by reconstructing the circumstances of its composition and its social and political significance.[5]

All of these approaches, however, attempt to excuse or defend Lydgate's poetry by qualifying it in terms of the external conditions of his age. While to some extent these methods, particularly the recent historical investigations, have increased our understanding of Lydgate, they leave unanswered many questions about the nature of his poetry and his particular aims and purposes as a poet. In undertaking a new study of Lydgate, it is perhaps useful to begin with these concerns and consider his poetry from the point of view of the ideals and assumptions which underlie it. As Lydgate's numerous digressions about poetry make clear, he conceives of poetry in terms that are very different from Chaucer's on the one hand and the Renaissance poets on the other. For Lydgate, the poet is preeminently a craftsman who illuminates and adorns his matter. His effort joins wisdom and eloquence to engender goodness and lead man to truth. The poet's language forms an integral part of this process, and his high style, a feature of Lydgate's writing that has disturbed his critics, is the medium which Lydgate envisions as most appropriate to the noble purpose he attributes to the poet. Finally, Lydgate's vision of poetry manifests itself in specific political terms as he links the heightened language of poetry with the effectiveness of the order and harmony of the state.

The present study will thus reconsider the nature of Lydgate's poetry in terms of the traditions and ideals of poetry which it embodies. In examining the various kinds of poems he undertakes—courtly, didactic, religious, satirical, humorous, public and official—from this point of view, we gain a better sense of Lydgate's importance. Although his poetry is not always successful, his efforts considerably influence the poets who follow him and introduce the artistic and thematic concerns that dominate the fifteenth century. In reassessing Lydgate's poems in terms of their own aims and purposes, we may discover why his contemporaries admired him and, from this perspective, find him still to be an interesting poet today.

Lois A. Ebin

Barnard College

Chronology

ca. 1370	Lydgate born in Lydgate (or Lidgate), a village in Suffolk on the Cambridgeshire border.
1382	By this date Lydgate is recruited to the Abbey of Bury St. Edmunds where he remained with intervals until his death.
1389	13 March, ordained "ad omnes ordines" in the church of Hadham, near Bishop's Stortford. 17 December, receives letters dismissory for the orders of subdeacon.
1393	28 May, receives letters dismissory for the order of deacon.
1397	4 April, receives letters dismissory for the order of priest. 7 April, ordained priest by John Fordham, bishop of Ely.
ca. 1400–1402	*Flour of Curtesye, Complaint of the Black Knight.*
ca. 1403	*Temple of Glas.*
1406–1408	*Resoun and Sensuallyte.* Student at Oxford, probably at Gloucester Hall.
1409–1411	*Life of Our Lady.* (Schick dates this poem 1409–11; some modern editors place it 1421–22, and Norton-Smith suggests after 1434.)
1412–1420	*Troy Book* commissioned by Henry V.
ca. 1414–1417	*Ballade at the Departing of Thomas Chaucer into France.*
ca. 1420–1422	*Siege of Thebes.*
1420–1434	Lydgate is closely connected with the royal court; spends time in Paris and in London, Windsor, and Bury.
1422–1423	*On Gloucester's Approaching Marriage.*
1423	Elected prior of Hatfield Broadoak.
ca. 1424	*Mumming at Eltham.*

1424–1426	*Guy of Warwick, Danse Macabre, Title and Pedigree of Henry VI.*
ca. 1426–1430	*The Pilgrimage of the Life of Man.*
1427	*Mumming at London.*
1429–1430	*Legend of St. Margaret, Roundel for the Coronation of Henry VI, Mumming for the Mercers, Mumming for the Goldsmiths, Mumming at Windsor, Mumming at Hertford.*
1431–1439	*Fall of Princes.*
1432	*Ordenaunces for the Kyng made in the Cite of London.*
1434	*The Lives of St. Edmund and St. Fremund* presented to Henry VI during his visit to Bury St. Edmunds.
1439	*The Lyfe of Seint Alban and the Lyfe of Seint Amphabel.* 22 April, awarded a life grant of ten marks per annum from the customs of Ipswich.
1441	*Verses for Queen Margaret's Entry into London.* 1445 (?) *Testament.*
ca. 1446	Translation and adaptation of the *Secreta Secretorum* (unfinished).
1449–1450	Lydgate dies and is buried in the Abbey of Bury St. Edmunds.

Chapter One

John Lydgate: Monk of Bury

Lydgate's Life

Lydgate's origins in the village of Lydgate or Lidgate in Suffolk, on the Cambridgeshire border, were inauspicious and hardly presaged the role he would play for half a century as an important religious and secular poet. Born ca. 1370 of peasant stock, he spent the first twelve or thirteen years of his life in the quiet village just six miles southwest of Bury St. Edmunds where he would dwell for the major portion of his days in very different circumstances. Here, Lydgate claims in his *Testament,* he lived the life of an unschooled, wanton, and undisciplined youth.[1] Between 1382 and 1385, however, Lydgate came to the attention of one of the monastic officials and was recruited to the Abbey of St. Edmunds to begin a career in the priesthood. According to his account in the *Testament,* at first only his outward appearance changed, for although he donned the Benedictine habit, he remained reckless and disobedient within, scornful of the monastic rules: "Like the image of Pygmalion, / Shewed lyfly, and was made but of ston" (*Testament,* ll. 676–97). But after a vision near the age of fifteen, Lydgate reports, he put aside his youthful ways and devoted himself to the service of the order.

Although it is often difficult to separate fiction from fact in the *Testament,* we do know from other sources that in approximately 1385 Lydgate entered the monastery at Bury St. Edmunds as a novice. On 13 March 1389 he was ordained "ad omnes ordines" in the lowest of the four orders of the church at Hadham, near Bishop's Stortford.[2] On 17 December 1389 he received letters dismissory for the order of subdeacon, the first of the three major or sacred orders. Four years later, on 28 May 1393, he was raised to the order of deacon and in April 1397 he was finally ordained priest by John Fordham, bishop of Ely.[3] During his period as initiate, Lydgate was educated first in Latin grammar, the Scriptures and the liturgy, and then in the studies of the trivium—grammar, logic, and rhetoric—as well as the skills of formal writing and illumination.

Shortly after he was ordained as priest, in approximately 1400, Lydgate began his literary career. Among his early poems are several Chaucerian imitations, including "The Complaint of the Black Knight," "The Flour of Curtesye" (1400–1402?), and the "Temple of Glas" (1403?). Although we have very few records of Lydgate's activities during the early 1400s, we know from a letter of the Prince of Wales, later Henry V, addressed to the abbot of Bury that Lydgate was a student at Oxford between 1406 and 1408, probably at Gloucester College where the Benedictines sent their pupils.[4] According to an entry in MS. Ashmole 59 by John Shirley, the famous London copyist and an acquaintance of Lydgate's, Lydgate wrote his version of Aesop's *Fables* while he was in residence at Oxford at this time.[5] From the early 1400s also date *Resoun and Sensuallyte,* modeled on the French *Les Échecs Amoreux,* and possibly *The Life of Our Lady,* Lydgate's lengthy and eloquent devotional poem.

Lydgate, however, wrote his major works between 1412 and 1440 when he not only was associated with the monastery of Bury St. Edmunds, but also was closely connected with the royal court and a number of important English families as an official poet and rhetorician who might be called upon to write for various occasions. During this period, Lydgate produced three long secular narratives—the *Troy Book,* begun in 1412 at the command of Henry, Prince of Wales, and finished in 1420; the *Siege of Thebes* (1420–22?); and the *Fall of Princes,* written for Humphrey, duke of Gloucester—several significant religious works, saints' lives, and lyrics, including an account of the *Legend of St. Edmund and Fremund,* written at the request of Abbot Curteys for King Henry VI on the occasion of his three-month visit to Bury St. Edmunds.

Between 1420 and 1434, Lydgate spent a considerable portion of his time away from Bury St. Edmunds both in other parts of England and on the Continent. A record in the minutes of the Privy Council dated 21 February 1423 reveals that Lydgate was given a grant of land and, in June of the same year, was elected prior of Hatfield Broadoak in Essex, near Bishop's Stortford, a small priory recently attached to Bury.[6] The post, a sinecure, appears to have occupied Lydgate's attention as his principal residence between 1423 and 1426. From 1426 to 1429, Lydgate lived in Paris, in the train of the duke of Bedford, where he wrote at least two important poems, the *Danse Macabre* and *The Pilgrimage of the Life of Man.*[7]

During the next five years, he was back in England, in London, Windsor, and Bury. By 1432, Lydgate appears to have relinquished the priorate of Hatfield, and on 8 April 1434 he received official license to leave Hatfield and return to Bury where he remained for the rest of his life.[8] At Bury, Lydgate continued to receive commissions and grants for his writing, and in 1445–46 he undertook two long poems, the *Testament,* a retrospective confession, and the *Secreta Secretorum,* which remains unfinished. The last official notice we have of Lydgate's activities is in 1449 at Michaelmass when he drew his royal grant for the final time.[9] Shortly afterward, either in 1449 or early 1450, Lydgate died and was buried in the Abbey of Bury St. Edmunds.

The Abbey of Bury St. Edmunds

In the minds of many of his contemporaries and immediate successors, Lydgate's name was linked inseparably with his role as a monk, especially a monk of Bury. Associating Lydgate with the great English poets in his "Lament for the Makaris," Dunbar refers to "The noble Chaucer, of makiris flour, / The Monk of Bery, and Gower, all thre. . . ."[10] Similarly, Hawes, in *The Conforte of Louers,* speaks of Lydgate as "the monke commendable,"[11] while Skelton joins "Gower, that first garnished our English rude, / And Master Chaucer, that nobly enterprised / How that our English might freshely be enewed" with "The Monk of Bury then after them ensued, / Dan John Lydgate. . . ."[12]

A look at the history of the abbey and its position in Lydgate's time makes clear the importance of the poet's connection with the house of Bury St. Edmunds. One of the five richest Benedictine houses in England, the abbey developed into a center of political and intellectual activity with close ties in the fifteenth century to the kings and influential noblemen. With a church comparable in size to the impressive Durham Cathedral, the monastery dominated the town and surrounding countryside. Its extensive land holdings provided considerable wealth while its associations with the court brought many of its members into the larger world around them. For Lydgate, the Abbey of Bury St. Edmunds afforded a position of privilege as a writer, a secure base from which he could work, yet one which insured his contact with some of the most influential men and women of his time.

From as early as the seventh century, the site of the abbey was in religious use, housing a community founded ca. 633 by King Sigebert, the first Christian king of the East Angles.[13] In 903, the remains of King Edmund, martyred by the Danes at Haegelisdun (Hellesdon by Norwich), were brought to Bury. According to local legend, Edmund had been slain by Danish arrows and decapitated. His body was recovered, but his head eluded his followers until, by a miracle, they discovered a wolf crying "here," leading them to the spot where the saint's head had been hidden. After the renewal of Danish raids, St. Edmund's body was taken to London for safety in 1010 where it remained for three years.[14] A second miracle, the sudden death "by the Saint's spear" of the impious King Sweyn who made demands for ransom from St. Edmund's lands, provoked Sweyn's son, King Canute, to add generously to the Church of St. Mary on the site. In 1020, the monastery was founded and granted freedom from episcopal control, and twenty monks were substituted for the secular priests. Again, after the Norman Conquest, the freedom of the abbey was confirmed by William the Conqueror, who rebuffed Bishop Arfast's attempt to turn the abbey church into his cathedral.[15]

The first period of greatness for the abbey occurred under Abbot Baldwin (1065–97), who began an ambitious program of building, leveling the ancient timber church and laying the walls and foundation for the massive new abbey. Even more significant expansion took place under the supervision of the great Abbot Samson (subsacrist, 1180–82; abbot, 1182–1210) whose activities are recorded in detail by the chronicler Jocelin de Bracelond. From Jocelin's account, we learn that Samson took over the monastery when it was in debt and disorder, restored finances, enlarged the abbey's estates, and safeguarded its prosperity.[16] Several of Jocelin's anecdotes reveal Samson's ingenuity and ambition in establishing Bury St. Edmunds as one of the great centers of the period. Jocelin, for example, describes how Samson cleverly tricked his competitor in building, Geoffrey Ridell, bishop of Ely, who sought to obtain prime local timber for his carpenters to cut. The bishop's messenger, however, made a slip of the tongue in delivering his message, requesting timber of Elmswell when he should have said Elmset. Samson, realizing the error, eagerly granted the request, but after the messenger departed: "went at once with his carpenters to the aforesaid wood and caused all the oaks already marked together with more than a hundred others to be marked with his mark for the use of St. Edmund and for the top of the great tower; and he gave orders that they should be cut down as soon as possible."[17] As a result, before the bishop discovered the mistake, all of the trees were removed. "And so," Jocelin concludes, "he would have to find other timber elsewhere, if he wanted any." "Thus guile is tricked by guile."[18]

Samson's rule as abbot, however, was important not only for his building activity but for the ties he established between the monastery and the crown. As a close friend of both Henry II and Richard I, Samson involved the abbey in the political struggles of the time. In 1181, when Henry II visited Bury, according to Jocelin, Samson even requested permission to accompany the king on the crusade but was prevented from taking this risk.[19] Likewise, when Richard I was taken prisoner in Germany, Samson was instrumental in raising the required ransom money and journeyed to console the captive king.

After Samson's death, the monastery became involved in a conflict with Richard's successor, King John, and played a significant part in consolidating the earls and barons opposed to John's rule. On 20 November 1214 these men convened in the abbey church to hear Archbishop Langton read Henry I's charter. Each swore on the high altar that unless John granted them similar liberties they would go to war against him. Their threat led eventually to the sealing of the Magna Carta by John on 15 June 1215. In the remainder of the thirteenth century, the abbey also reasserted its power over the town. Originally the town of Bury was in the abbey's "liberty" or jurisdiction with full authority granted to the abbey over gates and tolls and the selection of town officials. The numerous disputes between the townspeople and the abbey about these privileges came to a head in the riots of 1327 when the townspeople invaded the abbey, plundered and burned many of its buildings, kidnapped the abbot, and attempted to obtain civic independence. Although they retained the upper hand briefly, the abbey regained control and considerable monetary recompense after order was restored by Edward III.[20] Again in 1381, the year of the Peasant's Revolt, the townspeople plundered the abbey, murdered the prior of Bury, John of Cambridge, and Sir John Cavendish, the chief justice. As a result the town was outlawed and fined 2,000 marks.[21]

In contrast to the turmoil and conflicts of the fourteenth century, the first half of the fifteenth century, the period of Lydgate's major poems, was a time of marked order and prosperity for the monastery. St. Edmunds during these years had the resources of a powerful corporation with considerable independence. Under the leadership of Abbot William Curteys (1429–46), a staunch defender of abbatical privilege, the monastery consolidated its holdings and authority in the region. Its income more than doubled between the end of the thirteenth century and the beginning of the fifteenth century while the number of monks increased to sixty or eighty from the forty-seven who survived the ravages of the Black Death.[22]

Like Abbot Samson before him, Curteys maintained close links with the royal court. A good example of the esteem that Henry VI revealed for the abbot is provided by his visit to the monastery in 1433–34. Although it was common for guests, including members of the royal family, to be housed at the monastery, Henry's extended stay from Christmas 1433 to Easter 1434 was unprecedented and is a significant indication of Curteys's favor. The accounts of the visit from Curteys's register of the event reveal the considerable preparations and expense the monastery took for the king.[23] As Lydgate indicates in his first book, it was in commemoration of the king's visit that Curteys asked him to write his *Life of St. Edmund.*[24] The dedication copy of the *Life* (Harley MS. 2278), an elaborately illuminated manuscript, contains a miniature that shows Lydgate kneeling before the shrine of St. Edmund and delivering his work to King Henry. In addition to his visits, the king frequently approached Curteys for advice and financial support.[25]

The Abbey of Bury St. Edmunds occupied an important position in Lydgate's day. Admission to the fraternity of the abbey was a considerable honor, bestowed under Curteys's rule to the king himself and a select group of noble men and women.[26] For the monks who served the abbey, monastic life offered a career of security and privilege. Their existence was not a remote and cloistered one; rather, the monks of the most powerful houses like Bury had access to important political, social, and intellectual circles in the court, the government, and the university.

Lydgate's Position as Monk and Poet

Lydgate's position as a "monk of Bury" in the fifteenth century brought with it certain advantages for him as a writer. In an age when books were costly and private collections of substantial size rare, the abbey provided Lydgate with a library of over 2,000 volumes renowned as one of the largest in England. The majority of the volumes in the Bury library were texts of the Scriptures and books of patristic commentary. In addition to separate texts of the books of the Old and New Testaments, the Bury library had copies of the writings of many of the important church fathers. From the patient studies of M. R. James, we learn that the Bury collection also contained many works of more explicit literary value—texts of the major Latin writers, Caesar, Cicero, Virgil, Horace, Ovid, Juvenal, Persius, Quintilian, Sallust, Statius, Suetonius, Seneca, Martianus Capella, Prudentius, and Valerius Maximus; medieval Latin historians and moralists, including William of Malmesbury, John of Salisbury, Giraldus Cambrensis, and two copies of Guido della Colonna's *Bellum Troianum,* the source of Lydgate's *Troy Book;* and a certain number of French and Old English homilies, sermons, and proverbs.[27] Many of the books were probably produced in the abbey itself for the use of the monks and some of them, for example, the splendid Bury Bible, copied and illuminated at the abbey between 1121 and 1148, and the presentation copy of Lydgate's *Life of St. Edmund,* Harley MS. 2278, were masterpieces of medieval manuscript illumination. Pynson's representation of Lydgate at his writing desk in his edition of the *Testament* suggests that Lydgate had the privilege of working in a private study or scriptorium where he might have composed his poems and kept some of his own volumes.[28]

Perhaps even more significant for Lydgate's career as a writer than the resources of books at Bury were the opportunities the monastery provided for contacts with the leading intellectual, political, and social figures of the day. During his tenure as a monk, Lydgate was closely acquainted with many important men and women, including members of the royal family, who became his patrons and supporters. The majority of his long works, in fact, were commissioned by the patrons who developed from his contacts through the monastery, and, in both the range of his support and in the number and variety of his patrons, Lydgate stands out from his English predecessors.

Shortly before Lydgate began his career as a poet, the control of patronage began to shift from a small court circle to a broader group of nobility and prominent members of the rising burgher class. The court audience of Richard II's reign, with its familiarity with French literature and its appreciation of Chaucerian irony and wit, gradually gave way in the fifteenth century to a reading public that was broader and more pragmatic in its tastes. As his career developed, Lydgate maintained ties not only with his royal sponsors, but increasingly with the groups of nobles and bourgeois who were interested in commissioning poems and translations of literary works. It is possible that his first important poem, *The Temple of Glas* (ca. 1403), received its support from this new class of patrons, for, according to Shirley, it was written "a la request d'un amoreux" to celebrate the union between a knight and his lady.[29] Since the motto of the lady praised in the poem is the same as that of the Pastons, *de mieulx en mieulx,* some critics have speculated that the poem might have been commissioned by this family.[30] During the same period, Lydgate also begins an association with Prince Hal, the future King Henry V, which would develop into a close relation between the poet-monk and the Lancastrian dynasty. As Schirmer points out, Lydgate and the monks of Bury were supporters of Henry IV, whom they viewed as an enemy of the Lollards. Henry, he speculates, might have encouraged his son Hal, as an act of favor toward the monastery which would strengthen its ties with the crown, to commission Lydgate to write the *Life of Our Lady.*[31] The completion of the book is represented in several manuscript illustrations with Lydgate kneeling amid ecclesiastical and secular officials, offering the *Life* to Prince Hal, who is seated on a throne.[32] On 31 October 1412 Hal encouraged Lydgate to undertake a second major work, a version of the Troy legend, which he viewed as a model of true chivalric deeds. Echoing Henry's interest in the envoy, Lydgate defends the king's French conquests and the validity of his claim to the throne and anticipates the union of the two countries in an age of true chivalry and peace.[33] During the remainder of his career, Lydgate would repeat both his homage and his advice in poems commissioned for numerous official occasions, including the coronations of Henry VI at Westminster and at Paris, the triumphal entry of the king into London on his return from France in 1432, the visit of the king to Bury St. Edmunds in 1433–34, the marriage of Henry VI to Margaret of Anjou, and in several nonoccasional religious poems for Queen Katherine.

Another important circle of Lydgate's patrons evolved from the household of Thomas Chaucer, the wealthy country gentleman and son of the poet. Thomas, who enjoyed the favor of the Lancastrian rulers, was sheriff of Oxfordshire and Berkshire, and in 1407 Speaker of the House of Commons for Oxfordshire. His home in Ewelme in Oxfordshire in the early fifteenth century was a center of social and cultural activity for figures like Humphrey of Gloucester, John Tiptoft, Thomas Montacute, William de la Pole, and William Moleyns, who, in many cases, in turn became Lydgate's patrons. Thomas's daughter, Alice, like her father, was a supporter of Lydgate's work and her second husband, Thomas Montacute, the earl of Salisbury, commissioned Lydgate's translation of Deguileville's *Pélerinage de la vie humaine,* while her third husband, William de la Pole, duke of Suffolk, ordered Lydgate to compose his *Virtues of the Mass* for his household.[34]

After 1422, Humphrey of Gloucester, the brother of Henry V and a powerful political figure, sought Lydgate's poetic services.[35] Humphrey first commissioned Lydgate to write a poem in celebration of his marriage to Jacqueline of Hainault and Holland, a sensitive political issue that threatened to strain the Anglo-Burgundian alliance and the basis of Bedford's policy of peace with France. More important was Gloucester's role in initiating and supervising Lydgate's translation of the *Fall of Princes.* Humphrey not only commissioned the work, but apparently lent Lydgate a number of books from his library for the purposes of amplifying the original text.[36]

Finally, Lydgate benefited from a number of important women patronesses, including Margaret, Lady Talbot, and later countess of Shrewsbury, for whom he wrote *Guy of Warwick* between 1423 and 1426, and Lady March, the sponsor of his version of the *Legend of St. Margaret.* His renown was considerable during the second half of his career and his work was in demand simultaneously by the crown, the nobility, and the bourgeoise. His minor poems include a sampling of the extremes of his patrons' requests, ranging from the exquisite religious poems for Queen Katherine to the mummings written for specific occasions for noble families and, in some cases, for various guilds and groups of burghers, to the mundane "Treatise for Lavenders" commissioned by Lady Sibille Boys of Holm Hale, which instructs her laundresses how to care for her attire.[37] The diversity of his patronage suggests the considerable esteem in which the monk of Bury was held in his day.

The Historical and Political Background of Lydgate's Poetry

The requests of Lydgate's patrons often involved him in the significant historical and political events of the time as commentator and propagandist. The beginning of his career coincided roughly with an event that had far-reaching repercussions in the period—the overthrow of the legitimate king, Richard II, by Bolingbroke, the future Henry IV, and the introduction of the Lancastrian dynasty that was to dominate English government for the next century. The conflicts that culminated in this act were deep-rooted and long-standing. When Edward III died in 1377, he left his grandson Richard II a country on the verge of civil war. At home, dissatisfaction about oppressive social conditions was increasing while abroad England was involved in a conflict with France that at that time appeared to have little hope of being resolved successfully. Richard came to the throne as a child of ten years and the early part of his reign was dominated by a Regency Council which essentially proved to be a continuation of the rule of his uncle, John of Gaunt. Under this regime and later under Richard's personal rule, a number of harsh measures antagonized the people and, in January 1396, Richard sacrificed the little popular support that remained by marrying Isabella, daughter of King Charles VI of France, and pursuing a policy of reconciliation with France. In an effort to tighten his control over the country, he had his enemies disinherited and exiled or condemned to death and executed as traitors. The twenty-two months of his kingship that followed were characterized by despotic rule.

When Richard's cousin, Henry Bolingbroke, sailed from Boulogne in June 1399 to recover his inheritance to the Duchy of Lancaster after the death of his father, John of Gaunt, the time was ripe for change. While some chroniclers assert that Henry planned only to recover his rightful estates, others claim that he had the larger goal of kingship in mind, an ambition that was reinforced by the overwhelming number of supporters who joined his cause.[38] According to the chronicler Adam of Usk, as Henry made his way from the north to London, his adherents swelled in number to 30,000, and by the time he reached Gloucester he headed an army of about 100,000.[39] After the submission of many of his followers, Richard abdicated the throne on 29 September, and on the following day Henry claimed the kingship. The official accounts of the proceedings given in the Parliament rolls suggest that Richard abdicated willingly without any protest.[40] However, the Dieulacres Chronicle and the Whalley Continuator of the *Polichronicon* assert that Richard acted under coercion, responding to the commissioners who visited him in the Tower that he "should not enter parliament in horrible fashion, as it was said, and placing the crown of the kingdom upon the ground he resigned his right to God."[41]

Before an assembly convened on 30 September, the report of the committee of deposition was heard and accepted and Henry's challenge of the crown approved. The decision was followed by an *electio in regem* in which the people of London acclaimed Henry as king and an elaborate coronation followed on 13 October. Despite Henry's efforts to legitimize his title and consolidate his support in the realm, after the mysterious death of Richard (ca. January 1400) sentiment in favor of the deceased king surfaced, especially in the north and in the midlands. When Henry V took over as king in 1413, anti-Lancastrian feelings remained among some nobles and in a more serious and threatening form among the increasingly vocal group of Lollards who opposed the Lancastrian policy and briefly rebelled after the trial of their leader, Sir John Oldcastle, in 1414.

As poet and friend of Prince Hal, Lydgate was called into service in the *Troy Book* to articulate the ideals for which Henry stood—true chivalry in defense of his country, honorable peace, and justice. The pictures he paints of the king through the figures of Hector and Troilus and the portrait in his envoy accord with the views that run through the contemporary *Gesta Henrici Ouintici* (1413–16) and with the ideals set forth in the king's official documents.[42] Lydgate introduces Henry as a hero-king, "of knȝthod sours & welle" (*TB,* envoy, l. 1) whose fame is spread throughout the world.

> Most worþi prince, of knyȝthod sours and welle,
> Whos hiȝe reoun þoruȝ þe world doþ shine,
> And alle oþer in manhood dost excelle,
> Of merit egal to þe worþi nyne,
> And born also by discent of lyne
> As riȝtful eyr by title to atteyne,
> To bere a crown of worþi rewmys tweyne!
> (*TB,* envoy, ll. 1–7)

Henry is prudent and firm, wise and merciful, yet fierce against rebels; like David in "kyngly pite," but like Caesar in battle. In his person, he combines the virtues of the sword and the scepter; he is, in sum, a model of the strong and just king.

The writing of the *Troy Book* also involved Lydgate in the controversies about Lancastrian foreign policy. As a result of the Treaty of Bretigny (or Calais), signed on 8 May 1360 under Edward III, England, in return for the renunciation of formal claim to the French throne, gained sovereignty over Calais and Ponthieu and title to Acquitania, Guienne, Perigord, and Gascony. In compensation for the renunciation of the treaty with Flanders, the French terminated their alliance with Scotland and agreed to pay England three million gold crowns for the ransom of King John. The calm following this settlement, however, did not last long. In 1369, the English resumed claim to the French throne and, after an unsuccessful campaign, their possessions in France were reduced. During the reign of Richard II, the conflict with France dragged on, finally coming to a standstill after the death of Charles V when the rulers in both England and France were minors.

When Henry IV came to the throne, he tried to avoid war by negotiating a marriage between Richard II's widow, Isabella, the daughter of Charles VI, and the Prince of Wales. But in France, civil war flared up and both the duke of Burgundy and Charles of Orleans sought English aid. Henry secretly negotiated with both parties, agreeing to the marriage of the Prince of Wales to Anne, the daughter of the duke of Burgundy, and continuing his dealings with the Orleanists who offered him Aquitania as an incentive to join their side.

In 1413, when his reign began, Henry V faced a difficult decision. He could either renew the English demands for the French crown or he could turn to the unfulfilled terms of the Treaty of Calais for sovereignty over the agreed upon portion of French land. Believing in his right to the French throne, Henry sought to conquer the country and then lead a united Christendom against the Turks. As Schirmer points out, Henry's desire for a French conquest as a prelude to a Crusade contrasts with the more pragmatic interpretation of some of his contemporaries, for example, the author of *The Lybelle of Englyshe Polyce* (ca. 1436–37), who considers Henry's plan in terms of its advantages for English commerce.[43] Hoccleve, however, who dedicates his *Regement of Princes* (1411–12) to Henry, articulates the king's idealistic view.[44] When Henry commissioned the *Troy Book* from Lydgate in 1412, he must have expected a similar endorsement of the English dual kingship, and, indeed, in the conclusion of his work Lydgate defends Henry's right to the French throne as he would later do for his son, Henry VI:

> He hath conquered his herytage ageyn
> And by his myȝti prudent gouernance
> Recored eke his trewe title of Fraunce;
> þat who-so liste loken and vnfolde
> þe pe-de-Grew of cronycles olde,
> And cerchen bokes y-write longe a-forn,
> He shal fynde þat he is iustly born
> To regne in Fraunce by lyneal discent.
> (*TB,* 5. 3384–91)

Lydgate's interpretation of Henry's dual kingship and his marriage to Katherine of France as a beginning of a golden age of peace represents a hope and vision rather than a reality; but he nevertheless introduces guarded criticism of the broader Lancastrian foreign policy that would be articulated more broadly in the *Siege of Thebes.* In July 1414 Henry demanded from the French the renewal of the treaty of 1360 and his ancient rights to the crown. As a first step, he proposed marriage with Princess Katherine and the territory of the kingdom of Anjou as a dowry. Despite the pledge of the dauphin and the Burgundians not to enter into an alliance with England, Burgundy concluded a secret agreement with the English on 28 September 1414 that resulted in the resumption of the war. In the summer of 1415, Henry arrived in France, immediately took Harfleur, and gradually made his way across the country. Finally, on 25 October, his victory at the Battle of Agincourt marked a turning point in the war and, like Edward III before him, enabled him to return to England in triumph.

After entering into a secret treaty with Emperor Sigismund of Germany in the following year, Henry invaded France for a second time, winning a decisive victory at Rouen. Peace negotiations resumed with Henry pressing his demands for the terms of the 1360 agreement and the territory it provided. But while the negotiations were in progress, the Burgundians and the Orleanists were reconciled in a formal treaty signed on 11 July 1419; in response, Henry conquered Pontoise while the English made a demonstration raid on Paris. After members of the Armagnac party murdered Duke John on the day set for his meeting with the dauphin, the situation turned suddenly in favor of the English. John's murder and the outraged response of the Burgundians led quickly to the settlement of the Treaty of Troyes, sealed on 21 May 1420. According to this treaty, Henry would marry Princess Katherine of France. While

Charles VI lived, he would remain king, but upon his death, the French crown would pass to the English king and his heirs forever. Since Charles was in ill health, however, Henry would act as regent with the counsel of the nobles and wise men of France and, in return, Henry undertook to subject all of France still under control of the dauphin. On 2 June, Henry married Princess Katherine and then moved rapidly to conquer Montereau and Melun. Finally, on 1 December 1420, he joined Charles and the duke of Burgundy on a triumphal entry into Paris and the next month left for England, landing in Dover on 1 February.

Although Henry had been victorious in France, the England he returned to was hard-pressed financially as a result of his campaigns. In the opening speech of the Parliament which convened on 2 December 1420 the chancellor had expressed the desire of the nation to have the king back, alluding to the poverty and distress of Henry's subjects and the general scarcity of money.[45] Upon his return, between the coronation of Queen Katherine on 24 February and the May Parliament, the king and the queen made a tour of the country. But their journey was interrupted by the news of Thomas, duke of Clarence's, defeat at Baugé on 21 March. Henry hurried back to France and again secured his position before he became ill and died on 31 August 1422 at Bois de Vincennes. According to contemporary accounts, he exhorted his followers—the duke of Bedford, his uncle Thomas Beaufort, Richard Beauchamp—on his death bed to continue the struggle until peace and "my rights" are granted, thus bequeathing to his infant son, Henry VI, the protracted war.[46]

Although many poets and chroniclers celebrated Henry's military victories with lavish praise, Lydgate responded to the conquests in France with more caution.[47] In his *Siege of Thebes* (1420–22), one of his few poems written without a commission, he reacts to Henry's foreign policy. Just as in ancient Thebes, so in contemporary England, he suggests, there is a divided view of the war effort. In the long debate between the opposing armies in part 3 of the poem, a section which he amplifies from his sources, one group expresses its discontent with the prolonged struggle and urges peace. The other supports war as a matter of honor and refuses to consider the wise Amphorax' counsel. The poet concludes that war benefits no one for it defeats both the conquered and the conqueror by destroying cities, towns, and people.[48] Directly incorporating in the poem the language of the recently concluded Treaty of Troyes, Lydgate expresses his desire for a policy of peace to end the long conflict.[49]

The hope which Lydgate introduces, in both the *Troy Book* and the *Siege of Thebes,* for a golden age of peace, however, was elusive. In addition to the renewed conflicts in France, the minority of Henry VI had to deal with dissension in England between the factions in the government headed by Henry Beaufort and Humphrey of Gloucester. By his will Henry had appointed his younger brother, Humphrey, regent in England. But in the first Parliament of the new reign, the magnates rejected Henry's plan, established the office of protector, a position of much more limited power for Humphrey, and set up a regency council in which Beaufort had the most significant role. The struggle between these two men for power and the attempts at mediation by John, duke of Bedford, Henry's regent in France and the husband of Anne of Burgundy, dominated the political scene during the minority of Henry VI.

At the same time, England's position in France continued to weaken as Joan of Arc led an army of French first to relieve Orleans, then to gain Patay, and finally to crown Charles VII king of France at Rheims. At Bedford's urging, Henry crossed the channel on St. George's Day, 1430, but was forced to delay for three months at Calais. Fortunately for him, during this time Joan of Arc was captured, sold to the English, and, on 29 May 1431 tried and burned at the stake. Although Henry VI was crowned king of France, after he returned to England the situation abroad again deteriorated while, at home, the conflict between Beaufort and Gloucester resumed. Both as a result of the strained economic and political conditions in England and the threat of Burgundian defection in France, Henry was forced to attempt to negotiate peace with the French. After an inconclusive series of meetings at Arras, the duke of Burgundy reconciled with Charles VII, thereby nullifying the Treaty of Troyes and jeopardizing the remaining English territories in France. In 1436, Paris fell, leaving the English with only Calais and Rouen. Again the two nations negotiated for peace with the English now ready to give in to most of the French terms at Arras. But in the conference at Gravelines, the French increased their demands and no agreement was concluded.

Lydgate reacts on several occasions to the conflict over Henry's minority. In addition to his numerous ballads and poems in celebration of official events, Lydgate comments explicitly on the danger of the political divisions that plague the realm in his only prose work, *The Serpent of Division,* which Schirmer argues belongs to this period.[50] Using the life of Caesar as an example, Lydgate emphasizes the horrors of civil war, arguing that a kingdom will be powerful only as long as it remains unified. A similar warning against division is more briefly articulated in the poem "A Praise of Peace," where Lydgate prays for peace between England and France, suggesting that peace causes abundance between brothers for their mutual benefit.[51] Lydgate's warnings, however, were more relevant than he realized at the time, for soon after his death, the dissension of Henry VI's reign erupted in the War of the Roses between the Lancastrian and the Yorkist parties. Both Gloucester and Suffolk, the old leaders of the opposing factions, fell from power, were arrested, prepared for trial, and mysteriously killed. The new adversaries who took their place, Richard of York and Edmund Beaufort, duke of Somerset, faced a powerless king in civil war. Likewise, the hopes Lydgate had in his poems for the French queens, Katherine of Valois (the wife of Henry V) and Margaret of Anjou (the bride of Henry VI), to mediate peace proved ill-founded. Katherine died in 1447 while Margaret aggravated the dissension in England by allying herself with Suffolk against the Gloucester faction. Lydgate, however, did not live to see the fruit of their pact or the collapse of the order he valued.

The Poet as Civilizer and Orderer

In his poetry, Lydgate responds to contemporary events with a vision of the poet as a civilizer and orderer of man. Underlying his major works is a recurrent thematic emphasis on the importance of peace and stability, the dangers of war, the threat of civil discord and division in the realm, and a recognition of the fragile and transitory nature of earthly order. Reviewing the events of the past from the perspective of fifteenth-century England, he underscores the need for stability in the nation and virtue and harmony in man's daily life. It is the poet's role to inspire man to this order and to lead him to wisdom and truth.

By his treatment of the myth of Amphion, the legendary founder of Thebes, which he introduces several times in his work, Lydgate elaborates this view and defines the relation between the poet, the language of poetry, and the state.[52] In the *Siege of Thebes,* he represents Amphion as the poet-king who founded the city of Thebes principally by the power of his words.[53] His language was so pleasing and appropriate that it brought order out of chaos and caused all to do his bidding in concord (sts. 231–33). Diverging from his source, Boccaccio's *De genealogia deorum,* for the myth, Lydgate draws the following moral: "the soote sugred harpe" of Mercury is more fortunate than the sword of Mars "whetted kene and sharpe."[54] Men may gain more by fair language than by war.

Developing his vision of the power of the poet-king Amphion's words, in the *Fall of Princes* Lydgate draws attention to the role of poetry as a deterrent to the destructive effect of Fortune, the force that threatens not only king and state, but all human civilization and order. Reworking Laurent de Premierfait's *Des Cas des Nobles Hommes et Femmes,* Lydgate sets up the story of Amphion as a frame to the crucial events of book 6 of the *Fall,* his account of the downfall of civilization represented by imperial Rome.[55] At the outset of the book, he inserts a reference to Amphion into the debate between Fortune and Boccaccio to underscore the role of eloquent language in reforming men and creating order (*FP,* 6.335–91). Like Amphion who civilized the Thebans by means of his "fair langage" and his "song" (*FP,* 6.335–41), Boccaccio as poet attempts to lead men to virtue which is removed from Fortune's domain. In defending his work against Fortune's challenge, he sets up an opposition between the power of poetry and the power of Fortune. While Fortune repeatedly brings disorder, strife, and discord, poetry and eloquence lead men back to a civilized and harmonious state. Again at the end of book 6, Lydgate departs from his source to introduce the example of Amphion as a reminder of the singular powers of eloquent language to bring concord and comfort:

> Bexaumple as Amphioun, with song & elloquence
> Bilte the wallis of Thebes the cite,
> He hadde of rethorik so gret subtilte.
> In his langage ther was so gret pleasaunce,
> Fynding therbi so inli gret proffit,
> That al the contre kam to his obeissaunce. . . .
> (*FP,* 6.3491–96)

In the body of book 6, Lydgate catalogs stories that reveal the destruction of civilization represented by imperial Rome through chaos, disorder, and the ravages of Fortune, beginning with the history of the Saturnine and ending with Caesar's conquest of Egypt, destruction of Alexandria, and death at the hands of Brutus. The examples end with the climactic story of Cicero, the "Laumpe and lanterne of Romeyn oratours," who restored concord to Rome. For a brief moment under his influence, the power of eloquent language reaffirms the harmony and order Fortune repeatedly seeks to destroy. Ultimately, however, Cicero is exiled and slain and the book ends with the beginning of a new cycle of war and disorder. By setting this account within the frame of the example of Amphion, Lydgate reminds the reader of the opposing forces of poetry and Fortuna and the continuing struggle of the poet, despite Fortuna's threats, to bring order and concord to men. Near the end of his long translation, he goes even further, emphasizing not only the poet's power but his sacred obligation to write:

> . . . he that can and ceseth for to write
> Notable exaumples of our predecessours,
> Of envie men wil hym atwite,
> That he in gardyns leet pershe þe holsum flours
> In sondry caas that myhte do gret socours. . . .
> (*FP*, 8.162–66)

As an orderer and civilizer of men in a mutable world, the poet has a responsibility to persist in his craft.

The conception of the poet as an orderer and enlightener of men also is reflected in the critical terminology Lydgate develops in his writing to define the qualities of good poetry. In his numerous digressions about poetry, he coins several words and popularizes other terms, which were used in English before but not to refer to poetry, to draw attention to an ideal of poetry as a process of illumination which enlightens man's mind and ennobles him.[56] His terms indicate that the poet is an "enluminer" who sheds beams of "rethorik" and "elloquence" on his matter, rendering it "aureate," "goldyn," and splendid. Like God, who "enlumines" the natural world with his light, the poet by his poetic light enables men to consider truths that otherwise would be hidden to their minds. Unlike many of his predecessors, who were anxious about the effect of the poet's rhetoric and eloquence and the power of poetry to lead men to truth, Lydgate asserts that the poet's activity is ennobling and that his language directs men to wisdom and virtue. In his vision of the poet and in his assumptions about poetry, Lydgate finally departs from his earlier English "maisters."

Chapter Two
The Courtly Poems

Aside from his translation of Aesop's *Fables* and a few minor didactic poems including *The Churl and the Bird* and *The Horse, Sheep, and Goose,*[1] Lydgate's first poetic endeavors are in the courtly mode. Largely influenced by Chaucer and the French love poets, Jean de Meun, Machaut, Deschamps, and Froissart, these works, as far as we can determine, date from the period before 1420 at the latest, and probably from between the years 1400 and 1412.[2] Most of the poems are occasional pieces, written to order for specific patrons, and although they differ in external circumstances, they share common themes, motifs, and images. Five of the poems—"A Complaynte of a Louers Lyfe," the "Floure of Curtesye," "A Gentlewoman's Lament," "A Complaint, for Lack of Mercy," and the *Temple of Glas*—are love complaints dealing with the themes of unrequited love and devotion. The remaining minor poems range from celebratory love poems to satirical denunciations of love, while *Resoun and Sensuallyte,* Lydgate's translation of the first 4,873 lines of the French *Les Échecs amoreux,* fuses courtly and moralistic allegory.[3] The number of manuscripts and prints that survive, at least eight each for the "Complaynte of a Louers Lyfe" and the *Temple of Glas* and two for *Resoun and Sensuallyte,* attests to the popularity of Lydgate's early courtly poems. Many of the pieces came to be attributed to Chaucer during the course of the fifteenth century or included in anthologies of Chaucerian poetry. But although Lydgate's early efforts are traditional in their themes, form, and mode and in the concerns they share with both Chaucer and the early fifteenth-century court poets, they finally depart from these works in ways that have a marked influence on the poetry of the remainder of the century.

The Courtly Complaint

Lydgate's relation to the courtly tradition is exemplified by his treatment of the familiar love complaint. The genre has a long history before the medieval period, with antecedents in Ovid's *Heroides* and Latin lyric and narrative. In the Middle Ages, the complaint, with its themes of desire and rejection, is incorporated into the structure of many love-lyrics. The lover's emotions generally are personified in the form of allegorical abstractions and his elaborate language acts as a form of "service" to the lady he desires. Words replace action as the underlying situation, the lover's plea for favor is amplified and embellished by the poet's rhetorical skill. In the works of the thirteenth- and fourteenth-century French poets, a sophisticated frame is added to the central complaint, characterizing in detail the narrator and the setting and, at times, linking the outer frame with the inner plea, for example, in the complaints of Machaut, Froissart, and Deschamps.

Chaucer turns to this tradition and to his immediate French models in his early complaints—*The Complaint of Venus,* the *Complaint to Pity,* and the *Complaint to his Lady.* These poems illustrate his skillful manipulation of the complaint genre in the familiar medieval form. But in the *Book of the Duchess,* the *Complaint of Mars,* and the *Anelida and Arcite,* he begins to experiment with the conventional mode by developing the connection between the frame and the central plea in terms of the psychological motives for the complaint and the relation between the poet-narrator in the opening section and the sorrowing lover in the central section. In the *Book of the Duchess,* and later in the *Troilus,* he increases the importance of the narrative elements and the relation of the frame to the complaint until the complaint itself is subsumed in the larger narrative frame. Finally, in the *Squire's Tale* and the *Franklin's Tale,* he exploits the much abbreviated complaint as a parody or distorting mirror of the work's themes.

Lydgate, in contrast, moves the complaint genre away from narrativity and realism toward artifact. Reducing the action to a minimum and severely restricting the range of his allegory, he narrows his focus to a single moment or moments in time. Rhetorically, he expands this moment, the complaint itself devoid of its familiar trappings, to create an intricate surface of words and sounds. The formal and stylistic devices, which he introduces to rework his traditional matter and transform emotion into design, become standard poetic practices of the period.

"The Complaint of the Black Knight"

Typical of his method at its best is one of his earliest poems, "The Complaint of the Black Knight," or, as it is titled by some of its scribes, "A Complaynte of a Louers Lyfe."[4] An extremely popular poem in the fifteenth century, the "Complaint" appears in eight manuscripts including a Shirley original (MS Add. 16165) and four Bodley manuscripts. In this poem, which draws heavily on Chaucer's *Book of the Duchess* and *Troilus* and the French love visions of Machaut, Deschamps, and Froissart, Lydgate begins with the conventional setting and imagery of the genre. The poet-narrator, suffering from a "sekenes sat ay so nygh myn hert" (l. 18), arises on a spring morning and goes out to find some remedy. Listening to the birds' song as the sun rises, he follows a river to a park complete with the conventional catalog of trees and flowers, delightful streams, and a well. Here he discovers a sorrowing knight dressed in black, whose complaint he overhears. The complaint includes the familiar descriptions of the lover's suffering, his bodily torment and woe, the allegorical battle of opposing forces for the lover, a description of the lady, her cruelty and attractions, and a concluding plea for mercy and a promise of service. The poem ends with the poet-narrator's desire to record the complaint he has witnessed and his prayer to Venus on behalf of true lovers.

But Lydgate transforms the conventional material he introduces by crafting his matter into a dense formal design. Large segments of the 680 lines of the poem are intricately woven networks of allusions. The seven-line opening stanza, a description of the spring season and setting, for example, echoes Chaucer's *Legend of Good Women* (1191), the *Troilus* (2.50–55), the *Merchant's Tale* (IV, E, 2220), the translations of the *Romance of the Rose* (2636–40), and the *Consolation of Philosophy* (3, m. 1).

In addition to his design of allusions, Lydgate embellishes his lines by several of his own peculiar syntactical and linguistic devices. Most prominent is his characteristic technique of word-pairing in which he typically joins a word or a phrase with one similar in meaning to increase the weight of his lines. Lydgate describes the water in the well in the frame of the poem as "so holsom and so vertuous" (l. 85). He explains that the Black Knight is of "colour pale and wan. / And wonder dedely also of his hiwe" and is suffering from "hurtes grene and fressh[e] woundes nyw" (ll. 131–33). Along with his device of reduplication, Lydgate frequently introduces the syntactical structure of a series of clauses loosely strung together to expand a particular passage. In the description of the Black Knight, for example, he amplifies the portrait by adding more than twenty such descriptive clauses before pausing (ll. 130ff.).

Finally, Lydgate extends his matter by means of new coinages. An impressive example of his tendency to move beyond the limits of his language and expand the range of his English is found in his description of the sunset near the end of the poem. In this passage, Lydgate first provides an elegant picture of the sun disappearing behind the horizon:

> And for because that hit drow to the nyght
> And that the sunne his ark divrnall
> Ipassed was so that his persaunt lyght,
> His bryght[e] bemes and his stremes all
> W[e]re in the wawes of the water fall,
> Vnder the bordure of our ocean
> His chare of gold his course so swyftly ran. . . .
> (ll. 589–95)

He then caps this description with the striking coinage "deaurat" ("gilded over") to represent the dramatic effect of the lingering rays of the sun at this moment: "And while the twilyght and the rowes rede / Of Phebus lyght wer deaurat a lyte. / A penne I toke . . ." (ll. 596–98). Likewise, in describing his lush surroundings at the outset of the poem, Lydgate coins the word "celured" ("covered over") to suggest the bower which nature creates to protect the flowers.

In "The Complaint of the Black Knight," Lydgate works the material he amplifies into an intricate formal design. Skillfully reorganizing the structure of the poem, he focuses maximal attention on the complaint itself. In the frame, which occupies approximately half of the stanzas, Lydgate creates a symmetrical pattern that leads us into and away from the knight's central lament. The poem opens with the sun's rising and closes with its setting. Parallel to this action is the narrator's awakening at the outset and his returning home to retire for bed at the end of the poem. In a third concentric circle, which frames the complaint itself, is the narrator's lovesickness and his inability to write and his recovery on both levels.

The patterning of the central section is even more complex. Lydgate develops the entire complaint as a striking network of structural and syntactical designs. Linking the frame and the lament, he begins by introducing a contrast between the sorrowing lover and his lush, springlike surroundings, between the "erber grene" "benched" with colors and the deadly pale knight in black (ll. 125–33). In the first four stanzas of the complaint that follow, Lydgate exploits a number of devices to create a dazzling surface of words and sounds. He carefully balances the lines of the description, reinforces this effect by parison, oxymoron, and other rhetorical figures, and finally locks each of these stanzas into place by concatenation:

> Now hote as fire, now colde as asshes dede,
> Now hote for cold, [now cold] for hete ageyn,
> Now colde as ise, now as coles rede
> For hete I bren; and this betwex[e] tweyn
> I possed am and al forcast in peyn;
> So that my[n] [hete], pleynly as I fele,
> Of greuous colde ys cause euerydele.
>
> This ys the colde of ynward high dysdeyn,
> Colde of dyspite and colde of cruel hate.
> This is the cold and euer doth besy peyn
> Ayen[e]s trouth to fight[en] and debate.
> (ll. 232–42)

In the next ten stanzas, Lydgate carefully groups the allegorical figures—which he introduces to represent the knight's distress—into opposing patterns, the good and bad military forces who wage war on the knight and the juristic figures who seek to undermine him with false accusations. The nine stanzas that follow embody contrasting catalogs which define another dimension of the knight's woe, the widespread injustice that prevails in love. Lydgate skillfully balances a list of true lovers unrequited with examples of false lovers rewarded. Finally, he caps this sequence with an even more intricately patterned conclusion in which he echoes the dramatic rhetoric of the *Troilus* epilogue by his emphatic syntactic repetition:

> Lo, how the fyne of lover[e]s seruise.
> Lo, how that Love can his seruantis quyte.
> Lo, how he can his feythful men dispise

To sle the trwe men and [þe] fals respite.
Lo, how he doth the swerde of sorow byte
In hertis such as must his lust obey
To save the fals and do the tr[e]we dey.
(ll. 400–406)

The effect of Lydgate's amplification and intricate patterning is to produce an elevated complaint in which language, style, and form are pushed beyond their traditional limits. The surface appeal of the structure Lydgate designs perhaps is seen most dramatically in the description of the *locus amoenus* at the outset of the poem. In his treatment of the landscape in stanzas 4–12, Lydgate plays upon the topos by representing the familiar aspects of the scene, the trees, flowers, and garden, transformed by the sun's intense light and the morning dew into a mosaic of silver and gold:

The dewe also lyk syluer in shynyng
Vpon the leves as eny bavme suete
Til firy Tytan with hys persuant hete

Had dried vp the lusty lycour new
Vpon the herbes in [the] grene mede,
And that the floures of mony dyuers hywe
Vpon [her] stalkes gunne for to sprede
And for to splay[en] out her leves on brede
Ageyn the sun golde-borned in hys spere
That dovn to hem cast hys bemes clere.
(ll. 26–35)

His alliteration and his unusual coinages like "golde-borned" reinforce the striking effect of his juxtaposed images. Under the influence of the poet's craft, nature is ordered, idealized, and transformed into part of the glittering design of the poem's surface.

"Floure of Curtesye"

In technique, the "Floure of Curtesye" forms a companion piece to the "Complaint of the Black Knight." The poem, of which there is no extant manuscript, first appeared in Thynne's 1532 edition of Chaucer and was attributed to Lydgate by John Stow.[5] Its style and meter correspond to Lydgate's practices in his early courtly period, and the work appears to be his on the basis of internal evidence.

Like the "Complaint of the Black Knight," the "Floure of Curtesye" turns its attention to the lady as an object of love and service. The poem begins on Valentine's eve as men and beasts alike prepare to serve love. Echoing Palamon and Arcite in the *Knight's Tale,* the narrator laments that while birds are free to choose their mates, man alone is constrained from his pleasure. Like these characters, he wonders "What meneth this? What is this purueyaunce / of God aboue, agayne al right of kynde, / Without[e] cause, so narowe man to bynde?" (ll. 68–70). Although he suffers from a love that will not succeed, he vows to remain loyal to the lady.

The remainder of the complaint, approximately 150 lines, is devoted to the poet-lover's praise of the lady as a creature of unsurpassed excellence. The poem moves from the traditional situation of praise to a celebration that is abstract and universal. The lady surpasses all models of excellence—the sun, the brightest of stars; the ruby, the most sovereign stone; the rose, the most beautiful of flowers. Lydgate systematically modifies the familiar catalog of the lady's attributes, generally a head to toe description of her beauty and her virtues, to form a catalog of nonvisual abstractions. The result is to universalize the lady as the object of the lover's adoration, to create by his crafting an abstract notion of excellence.

By framing the lady's portrait with a discussion of his activities as poet, the narrator draws further attention to the complaint as a process of crafting. Initially, he raises the problem of translating the lady's perfection into language and suggests that he is unworthy of the task. Finally, he vows to praise the lady in a still more elaborate form than the rime royal stanzas—the "ballade." In the last three stanzas of the poem, he fashions a difficult scheme of rhyme and echoing which he reproduces in each of the three stanzas of the ballade, thus completing the process of translating feeling into an abstract and stylized form.

By his conspicuous activity as poet, Lydgate thus links the complaint and idealization of the lady with the theme of the poet's effort to transmute emotion into artifact. The poem is fabricated from the matter of poetic tradition rather than the world of nature and represents a formalization or idealization of experience. Lydgate's direct allusions remind us that the poem's immediate referent is the love poetry of Chaucer—the *Parliament of Fowles* with its Valentine's Day celebration, the *Knight's Tale* from which the introductory dialogue is extracted, and the tales of the Franklin, the Clerk, and the Squire with their portraits of patient women. The "Floure's" process of abstraction is a response to Chaucer's poetic activity, to his creation of a literary language and tradition in English. Prefacing his closing ballade with an assessment of his master, Lydgate juxtaposes the eulogy of the lady, the model of excellence, with a celebration of Chaucer, the paragon of poets, thereby joining two examples of perfection:

> Chaucer is deed, that had such a name
> Of fayre makyng, that, without[en] wene,
> Fayrest in our tonge, as the laurer grene.
>
> We may assay for to countrefete
> His gay[e] style, but it wyl not be;
> The welle is drie, with the lycoure swete,
> Bothe of Clye and of Caliope. . . .
> (ll. 236–42)

The Short Courtly Lyrics

In the half-dozen short courtly poems that survive, Lydgate extends the range of his experimentation as a poet-craftsman. Although the poems are conventional in effect, many of them reveal the innovations that are apparent in more extended and striking form in the *Temple of Glas.* "My Lady Dere" and "A Lover's New Year's Gift" both develop the contrastive natural imagery that is central to the *Temple of Glas.*[6] In "My Lady Dere," the poet introduces the images of extreme darkness and extreme light to dramatize the effect of the lady on her lover. As Phebus chases away black clouds, so does the sight of the lady dispel the poet's sorrow. In a skillful series of stanzas, he associates the lover's feelings of elation at the sight of his lady with the spontaneous delight of the birds, animals, and plants in nature warmed by the sun. Returning to the light-dark imagery, he sums up the relation of the lover's moods to his lady's presence:

> Whanne Phebus doþe his bemys spred
> In somer, lyke as men may lere;
> So glad am I in thought and ded,
> Whanne þat I seo my lady der.

In somer whanne þe sheene sunne
Haþe shewed bright a gret space,
And towardes night þe skyes dunne
His clernesse doþe awey enchace;

Right so dedly and pale of face,
Mortal of look and eke of chere,
I wexe, suche wo me did enbrace
At partyng fro my lady der.
(ll. 85–96)

In "A Lover's New Year's Gift," Lydgate adds to this the image of the cloud that passes across the lover's mind in the absence of his lady. Introducing a catalog of women similar to the one in the "Floure of Curtesye," he celebrates the lady's unsurpassed excellence and concludes by offering her his heart and his poem as gifts or tokens of his devotion.

The remaining four poems are complaints, and, in each, Lydgate introduces a new twist or a small but skillful modification of the genre. In the "Ballade of her that Hath all Virtues," which Shirley suggests in Trinity MS. R.3.20 was written at the request of a squire "who served in love's court,"[7] and "The Servant of Cupyde Forsaken" or "Complaynt Lydegate," the poet shifts his stance in the concluding envoy and turns in the first poem from the lady's praise to a condemnation of her disdain and in the second, to a bitter denunciation of all women. In both the "Servant of Cupyde Forsaken" and "A Gentlewoman's Lament," Lydgate develops a personalized narrative voice that revitalizes the traditional complaint. The narrator of the "Servant" speaks as the perpetual loser in love, rejected both by high-born and by low, by the fair, the wealthy, the young and the old alike. In "A Gentlewoman's Lament," Lydgate turns to the female perspective, a perspective which becomes increasingly interesting to him in the various drafts of the *Temple of Glas*. In the woman's voice, he describes the plight of unrequited love of one of high estate. Skillfully expanding the traditional image of the love knot, he suggests the link between the lady and her lover, the bond that ties her memory to the lover, and the "knotting" of her heart in grief.[8]

The Temple of Glas

The *Temple of Glas* (ca. 1403) represents Lydgate's most fully developed complaint poem and the most ambitious of his efforts in the Chaucerian tradition. The poem, extremely popular in his day, appears in eight manuscripts, including Shirley's MS Add. 16165, Fairfax 16, Bodley 638, and Tanner 346.[9] The importance of the work to Lydgate is suggested not only by the care he lavished on the poem, but by the fact that it is the only long work that he wrote without the aid of an extended source. In this poem, Lydgate attempts to extend the complaint genre thematically as well as formally, creating a poem of greater substance and significance than any other of his early works.

Several changes are apparent in turning from the "Floure of Curtesye" and the short courtly complaints to the *Temple of Glas.* While the complaint occupies only a small portion of the stanzas in the "Floure of Curtesye" and about half of the stanzas in the "Black Knight," in the *Temple of Glas* Lydgate gives the complaint a new emphasis by assigning it more than two thirds of the lines of the poem. Moving beyond the skillful amplification of convention to experiment significantly with the genre itself, he devises a more innovative strategy to develop the complaint than we find in the other early poems. In contrast to his practice in these works, Lydgate introduces a double complaint in the *Temple of Glas* so that the poem embodies both the masculine and the feminine perspectives. Metrically, he demarcates the various structural sections by an alternating scheme of narrative couplets and rime royal stanzas which he substitutes for the unbroken rime royal or ballade stanzas of the earlier poems. The manipulation of couplet and rime royal divides the poem into two outer frame segments and three central sections, each followed by a brief passage of narrative.

Within this structure, Lydgate introduces an intricate system of oppositions to develop his theme, laying the foundation in two descriptive passages that he inserts in the opening lines of the poem. Echoing the *Hous of Fame,* he represents the narrator in bed:

> What þat Lucina wiþ hir pale liȝt
> Was ioyned last wiþ Phebus in Aquarie,
> Amyd Decembre, when of Ianuarie

Ther be kalendes of þe nwe yere,
And derk Diane, ihorned, noþing clere,
Had hir bemys vndir a mysty cloude. . . .
(ll. 4–9)

Suddenly, the narrator is "ravuysshed in spirit" to a temple of glass. Blinded by light, he cannot make out where he is until at last clouds form and mute the intense rays of the sun:

. . . the liȝt so in my face
Bigan to smyte, so persing euer in one
On euere part, where þat I gan gone,
That I ne myȝt noþing, as I would,
Abouen me considre and bihold
The wondre hestres, for briȝtnes of þe sonne;
Til at[te] last certein skyes donne,
Wiþ wind ichaced, haue her cours iwent
Tofore þe stremes of Titan and iblent,
So þat I myȝt, wiþin and withoute,
Whereso I walk, biholden me aboute. . . .
(ll. 24–34)

The two passages describe in turn the total absence of light in the darkest season of the year and the blinding excess of light reflected and refracted by the temple of glass. The system of light and dark images, which link the various segments of the poem, provide the vehicle for a successive redefinition of love, the central concern of the complaint genre.

The catalog of lovers with which the body of the poem opens suggests a view of love that contrasts with the vision Lydgate will develop at the center of the poem. Although critics have been puzzled by the composition of this catalog,[10] all of the lovers represented on the walls of the temple and the various lovers who petition to Venus are examples of the misfortunes of love, the "woe and pain" this state brings. Systematically, Lydgate groups the famous men and women who have suffered in love—Dido, Medea, Penelope, Alceste, Griselde, Paris, Achilles, Palamon—and the groups of contemporary plainants—the "þousands of louers" who report how they were exiled, rebuffed, slandered, betrayed, or paired against their desire.

In the central complaints, Lydgate qualifies this distressing vision by a successive enlargement of the view of love as the opposite of darkness and distress. Amid the array of people in the temple, the narrator discovers a lady kneeling in prayer and, as he describes her, he recalls the opening metaphors of light and darkness (ll. 251 ff.). But in contrast to the opening description, the lady possesses neither too much nor too little light. Rather by her presence, she "enlumynes" the temple around her. The lady's complaint and dialogue with Venus that follow develop the view of love as the antidote to suffering and pain. In the first seven rime royal stanzas, the lady addresses Venus as a beneficial source of light, the "devoider of derknes," the "cheif recounford after þe blak nyȝt" (ll. 329–30). She then describes her plight in five stanzas of contrasts without resolution, which seem to confirm the view provided by the frame:

> For I am bounde to þing þat I nold:
> Freli to chese þere lak I liberte,
> And so I want of þat myn hert[e] would,
> The bodi knyt, alþouȝe by þouȝt be fre;
> So þat I most, of necessite,
> Myn hertis lust outward contrarie—
> Thogh we be on, þe dede most varie.
> (ll. 335–41)

Venus responds by offering another definition of love which provides the resolution to the lady's conflicts. As she explains, "aftir a dropping mone" the weather clears and, when the storm is over, the "sonne shineþ in his spere briȝt" (ll. 394–96). People appreciate light more after they have been wrapped in darkness and good fortune after they have experienced bad. Thus Love first wounds and hurts his servants before he brings them to joy.

The notion that Love's pleasure can only be appreciated through its contrary is found in comic form in book 1 of the *Troilus* as Pandarus explains to the skeptical Troilus:

> By his contrarie is every thyng declared.
> For how myghte evere swetnesse han ben knowe
> To him that nevere tasted bitternesse?
> Ne no man may ben inly glad, I trowe,
> That nevere was in sorwe or som destresse.

> Eke whit by blak, by shame ek worthinesse,
> Ech set by other. . . .
>
> (*Troilus,* 1.637–43)

Behind this passage is a similar argument from the *Roman de la Rose* (21573–82) and finally from Boethius, book 4, prose 2, lines 10–17: "And of thise thinges, certes, everich of hem is declared and schewed by othere. For so as good and yvel ben two contraries, yif so be that good be stedfast, thanne scheweth the feblesse of yvel al opynly; and if thow knowe clerly the freelnesse of yvel, the stedfastnesse of good is knowen." Recalling the ideas in these passages, Lydgate translates this classification into a system that underlies both the structure and argument of the poem. In contrast to Chaucer, who allows the voices of Pandarus to intrude and the formalization of the scheme to break down, Lydgate pushes the imagery toward increased abstraction, exploiting the mode of opposites to encapsule or embody experience. When the lady replies to Venus in stanzas 20–26, the oppositions that dominated her first speech are gone and she now accepts Venus' definition of love. The climax of the section occurs in the last four rime royal stanzas as Venus drops green and white hawthorne branches, a symbol of constancy, into the lady's lap.

The man's encounter with Venus in the next section of the poem provides a specific example of what Venus has just taught the lady. Lydgate divides his long complaint into two parts, one in couplets and one in rime royal. The first part roughly corresponds to the initial complaint of the lady, but with some additions. Like the lady, the man describes his plight in terms of unresolved conflicts. He is bound when he would be free; he hangs in balance between hope and dread, pain and "glorie," life and death. But in the rime royal section of his speech, the man demonstrates his steadfastness despite his adversity and vows his unswerving devotion to the lady. Venus' response in stanzas 22 to 23 demonstrates the validity of her instruction to the lady and links her general statements to the man's specific case. Drawing together the images that have recurred in the poem, she reveals that joy will follow the man's suffering and love will reward him with his sweetness now that he has endured its bitterness "withoute grucching or rebellioun" (l. 879).

In the final rime royal section, the lovers vow their steadfastness and Venus joins them with a golden chain.[11] After reiterating the importance of constancy in love, she provides a climactic statement of the themes of the poem. The blinding light of the opening stanzas is now tempered and transferred to the lady, who will ease the man's heart "itroubled with derkness" (ll. 1208–11). After "al þe showres / Of his turment" (ll. 1215–16), the weather will clear. Venus caps her instruction with a final warning to avoid doubleness and then transforms the oppositions of the poem into a definition of love that reconciles all contraries:

> For white is whittir if it be set bi blak,
> And swete is swettir eftir bitternes,
> And falshode euer is drive and put abak
> Where trouþe is rotid withoute doubilnes.
> Wiþout[e] prefe may be no sikirnes
> Of loue or hate; and þerfor, of ȝow too
> Shal loue be more, þat it was bouȝt with wo.
> (ll. 1250–56)

An outburst of celestial song reinforces the harmony of Venus' resolution, and the rime royal stanzas end with a ballade, a still more ordered metrical form, in celebration of love.

Lydgate's formal and thematic developments in the *Temple of Glas* are the result of a substantial process of revision. As Norton-Smith has demonstrated, Lydgate reworked the poem at least three times.[12] The earliest version, found in Cambridge University MS. Gg. 4.27 and Shirley's MS Add. 16165, represents the lady and her complaint quite differently than in the later versions. In the early version, the Lady's complaint is conventional; she complains not about the frustration of true love, the theme of the later versions, but about "jealousye."[13] Initially, Lydgate is more interested in the man's complaint and in amplifying the rhetorical topoi he borrows. In the early versions, the Lady is dressed in black and red and her motto is *humblement magre.* Originally, the poem ends abruptly before the envoy with line 1379.

The second draft, contained in Fairfax 16 and Bodley 638, introduces the major feature of the finished poem—the new complaint—but lacks the details which attend this complaint in the final version. In the new complaint, the Lady decries her lack of freedom to set her heart where she will. She longs for another, but is subject and bound to a husband against her desire; she stands "departid even on tweyn" (l. 354). The second complaint thus introduces a perspective that is new to the English complaint—that of a woman who is unhappily married, yet virtuous, despite her love for another man.

The final version, which survives in Tanner MS. 346, changes several details which reinforce the themes of the new complaint. Developing the character of the Lady, Lydgate emphasizes her constancy and her humility. Norton-Smith points out that the new complaint will engage our sympathy only if the Lady is virtuous, at once faithful to her true love and honorable in marriage.[14] Thus, in the Tanner manuscript, Lydgate removes the three stanzas after line 495 in which the Lady seeks to revenge those jealous of her and her love, making her in the final version completely obedient to Venus' command. A similar motive underlies his changes in the color and flower symbolism. In the first version, Venus casts red and white flowers in the Lady's lap and then reminds her in a rather diffuse stanza that she is called Margaret and should be true and constant as the daisy, the flower that is always fresh. The red and white flowers are retained in Fairfax 16 and Bodley 638, but the allusion to Margaret with its associations with Alceste, a type of virtuous married love in Chaucer's *Legend of Good Women,* is omitted since it is no longer appropriate. In the Tanner manuscript, the flowers are changed to green and white hawthorne, a symbol of constancy, and these colors are, in turn, linked to a change in the lady's dress, now also green and white.

In the Tanner manuscript, Lydgate also provides a new motto, changing the *humblement magre* of the first version and the mixed motto of the second to *de mieulx en mieulx* at line 310 of the final version, and modifying this motto at line 530, he emphasizes a development of emotion in the resolution, *de mieulx en mieulx magre,* that is "better and better in spite of adversity."[15] Finally, Lydgate adds the envoy to create a more graceful ending in the second and third versions. The revisions, thus, reveal Lydgate's concern with the construction and coherence of the poem as he transforms the conventional complaint into a situation that extends the limits of the form in English.

Finally, Lydgate's originality in the *Temple of Glas* lies not in the small changes of conventional matter which critics have noted—the description of the temple of glass, the unique love triangle, or the introduction of "real suffering" into the world of the courtly complaint[16]—but in his thematic and formal innovations and in his amplification of the complaint form to make it suitable for a complex thematic development. In his early courtly poems, he develops models of amplification that are influential throughout the fifteenth century. The specific features of his amplificatory style, the peculiarly Lydgatian devices of reduplication of expression, exaggerated use of intensives, inverted word order, and the conspicuous series of loosely constructed clauses, become characteristic features of the expansive style of the period.

Resoun and Sensuallyte

In *Resoun and Sensuallyte,* which most critics also date in the early period before 1412, Lydgate turns his craft to a larger form and to a more sustained effort in the poetic techniques of the early lyrics. Like the courtly complaints, this poem is rooted in Chaucerian and French love-vision traditions. In translating the first 4,873 lines of his source, the French *Les Échecs amoureux,* Lydgate amplifies his material to more than 7,000 lines by his characteristic devices of reduplication, loosely connected clauses, and digressions. In embellishing the French poem, which is an encyclopediac mixture of practical advice, moralistic allegory, and love-vision lore, Lydgate uses every opportunity to exercise the stylistic and rhetorical skills for which poets later admired him. But although *Resoun and Sensuallyte* reveals an interest in amplification and poetic craft similar to the emphasis of the early courtly lyrics, it is, in many senses, a transitional poem for Lydgate, indicating a movement toward the long form and the manipulation of a primary sustained source which becomes a common practice in his poems between 1412 and 1422.

The poem survives in two manuscripts, Fairfax 16, which contains a number of poems by Chaucer and other poets, and MS Add. 29,729, a collection of poems either written by Lydgate or related to him.[17] The portion of the poem Lydgate translates begins with a brief humility topos and spring description. Amid the rejoicing of earth, animals, and man, Nature, the queen of all creation, appears to the narrator, reveals the extent of her domain, and instructs him. Scolding her charge for sleeping, she bids him to study the world and take the path to perfection. As she explains, man has two choices, the road to the east, the way of Reason, or the path to the west, the way of Sensuality. Warning the narrator of the dangers of sensuality uncontrolled by Reason, she urges him to hold to Reason's way. After she departs, the narrator begins his tour of the world and discovers four deities, whom he describes at length—Minerva, Juno, Venus, and Mercury—who represent respectively wisdom, riches, love, and eloquence. These deities recall the terms of the judgment of Paris, which the narrator is asked to review. Like Paris, he chooses the side of Venus who assures him that she is an ally of Nature and promises him a woman fairer than Helen. Venus introduces the narrator to her two sons, Deduyt (Pleasure) and Cupid, and advises him to seek the Garden of Pleasure. On his way to the garden, he passes through a forest of evergreen trees and unfading flowers where he encounters Diana, the goddess of chastity. With many examples of love's pain, Diana warns the narrator of the false pleasures of the garden of love and urges him to stay with her in the forest of chastity. But the narrator ignores her plea and continues his quest for the garden of pleasure, a garden which Lydgate describes with the familiar iconography of the *Romance of the Rose*—the walls, springs, birds, allegorical figures, well, fountain, and presiding deity, Cupid. After this vision, the narrator spies a lady playing chess with Deduyt and he learns that he is to be the next player. With much embellishment, Lydgate describes the chess board, interpreting each of the lady's pieces as one of her attributes. The poem breaks off after an account of the narrator's first four pawns.

The French version continues to describe the game of chess in which the poet-lover loses and is checkmated. Deduyt comforts the grieving narrator and leads him to Love, who takes him into his service, instructing him in the rules of the game. Strengthened, the poet challenges the lady to a new game of chess, but Pallas intervenes and admonishes him to devote his life not to sensuality but to more worthy goals—either to the contemplative life or to the active practical life. To this end, she offers the narrator thirty-five rules to cure him from the passion of love and then provides a considerable amount of practical advice about the various stations of human society and their appropriate behavior and duties, the institution of marriage, the upbringing and education of children, and the organization and management of the household. Finally, Pallas concludes with suggestions about earning and investing money. In his vast sweep, the French poet loses sight of his original focus and the reader emerges without the coherent allegory or philosophical overview of more skillful works like the *Romance of the Rose* or the *Complaint of Nature* from which the *Échecs* poet borrows.

Although Lydgate breaks off his version before the miscellaneous advice of Pallas, he appears to have been interested in translating *Les Échecs* for the opportunity it provided him to exercise his rhetorical skills and knowledge of classical myth in a didactic context. Contrary to his usual practice, Lydgate undertook the task on his own initiative, for the poem is one of only two of his many long works that is written without the support of a patron. In translating *Les Échecs,* Lydgate usually adds a considerable amount of material either of his own creation or from sources he repeatedly will turn to in later poems—the *Romance of the Rose,* the *Speculum naturale* of Vincent of Beauvais, Brunetto Latini's *Tresor, De Regimine Principum* of Aegiodo Colonna, and several of Chaucer's works. Thus, he expands the French author's rhetorical opening, embellishing, for example, his humility topos, description of spring, and portrait of Nature. With characteristically Lydgatian concern for the effect of the allegory, he greatly amplifies the portraits of the four deities, pausing to explain unclear details or allusions. In the case of Pallas, he methodically turns the classical details of his source to a clear Christian interpretation. Likewise, he expands many of the myths Diana relates to clarify their significance, for example, the stories of Venus and Adonis (ll. 3685 ff.) and Venus and Mars (ll. 3760 ff.). In the case of Pyramus and Thisbe (ll. 3954 ff.) and Icarus and Phaeton (ll. 4162 ff.), he extends the versions in his source to three or four times their original length. In dealing with the iconography of the Garden of Pleasure, Lydgate finds it necessary to elucidate the familiar scheme, suggesting that some of the details of Guillaume's and Jean's allegory might have lost their original impact. But it is in the action describing the game of chess that he adds the greatest amount of original material, amplifying the ninety-two lines of the French version to 776. Most interesting are his numerous digressions in praise of women, whom he celebrates after dealing with each pawn and the virtue it suggests as impressive representatives of these qualities. Lydgate's amplification of *Les Échecs* thus provides a compendium of allusions to earlier myth, classical and medieval learning, and literary tradition, as well as a storehouse of polished or crafted passages to be borrowed or echoed by later poets. Like Boccaccio in the *Genealogia deorum,* Lydgate assembles matter that is familiar but fading from view and refashions it in a form that insures its accessibility to later writers.

Although his beginnings in the early courtly poems are in the Chaucerian tradition, Lydgate turns from the concerns of his master to experiment with the themes, forms, and literary styles he borrows. Amplifying forms like the complaint by extending its stylized descriptions of emotion and its topoi of service and devotion, he moves the genre toward increased abstraction. By concentrating his attention on the surface of the poem, the pattern or design of the lines, and the interplay of imagery and allusion, he creates an attractive structure or artifact. His role in these poems is primarily that of craftsman who skillfully fashions the matter of his verse. Although in the *Temple of Glas* and *Les Échecs amoureux* he begins to move toward larger didactic designs, reassessing the central theme of the complaint, the view of love as suffering in the *Temple* and the allegorical choices of *Les Échecs,* his concern in these poems is still chiefly in the embellishment and extension of familiar matter. This view of the poet, however, will be redefined in the public poems which occupy Lydgate almost exclusively during the next ten years.

Chapter Three

Poetry and Politics: Troy and Thebes

In the minds of many of Lydgate's contemporaries, the two great epics, the fall of Troy and the siege of Thebes, were linked in terms of both their matter and their moral lessons. The two stories often appeared together in single manuscripts as reminders of the greatness and transitoriness of human order.[1] In Lydgate's own career, the *Troy Book* and the *Siege of Thebes* have an important position as public poems in which Lydgate first explicitly directs his skills as poet-craftsman to the concerns of the state. Linking the poet's special or heightened language with the political well-being of the state, Lydgate views the poet as an orderer and civilizer of men. Like the mythical figure of Amphion, the legendary founder of Thebes, the poet leads men to virtue by his eloquence and turns their attention to the peace and harmony of the realm.

The Tradition of Troy

In 1412, the year before he was to succeed to the throne as King Henry V, Henry, Prince of Wales, commissioned Lydgate to translate the story of Troy. As Lydgate explains in his prologue, Henry viewed the history of Troy as an example of true knighthood and chivalry for courageous men to imitate.[2] Traditionally, the story was held in special favor by the English, who traced their ancestry back to the Trojans exiled after the destruction of the city. This myth, which survived in the early Middle Ages, was embellished and popularized by Geoffrey of Monmouth in his *Historia Regum Britanniae* (1135) where he described the journey of Brutus from Troy to Britain, the founding of New Troy (London), and the succession of English kings.[3] Two centuries later, the vision still survived as the Gawain poet opened his romance—*Gawain and the Green Knight*—with a brief account of the English descent from their Trojan roots.[4] Because they associated themselves with the Trojans rather than the Greeks, the English and, to a large extent, the medieval audience preferred sources other than Homer's narratives which favored the defeated Trojan's enemies. Homer, in fact, was not well-known in the Middle Ages and generally was discredited as a historian. Guido delle Colonne, Lydgate's authority, asserts in his prologue that Homer deceived his readers by falsifying his matter and by reporting events that did not occur.[5] His errors in turn influenced Ovid and Virgil, whose accounts, Guido argues, must be dismissed as fictitious.

The preferred authorities for the medieval narratives of Troy were Dictys Cretensis and Dares Phyrgius, who, unlike Homer, were purported to have been eyewitnesses to the events. Dictys, a Cretan who fought at the siege of Troy, kept a soldier's journal in Phoenician characters which is said to have been buried with him and recovered after an earthquake opened the tomb during Nero's reign.[6] The journal, translated as *Ephemeris Belli Troiani* at the request of the emperor, actually was written in Latin in the fourth century A.D. from an earlier Greek version. It begins with an account of the arrival of the heirs of Atreus in Crete and, extending the scope of the Troy story, continues through the return of Odysseus. Dares, a Trojan eyewitness during the war, was believed in antiquity to have written a lost earlier *Iliad.* The surviving *De Excidio Troiae Historia* presents itself as a Latin translation of this work by Cornelius Nepos in what he calls "the straightforward and simple style of the Greek original," in fact, a rather poor Latin.[7] The *Historia* begins with the expedition of the Argonauts who destroyed Old Troy after being refused permission to land there by Lamedon, covers the events of the war and the destruction of New Troy, and ends with the sacrifice of Polyxena, the return of Helen, and the departure from Troy of Cassandra, Andromache, and Hecuba. Although this work covers twice as much material as the *Ephemeris,* it is only one fourth as long and is often extremely sketchy in its treatment. Its influence, however, was significant throughout the Middle Ages.

The works of Dares and Dictys were combined as sources in the *Roman de Troie* (1165) by the inventive Benoit de St. Maure, who turns the sketchy accounts of his originals into a full-fledged medieval romance.[8] Adding a considerable amount of new material, including the story of the love of Troilus and Briseyde (the ancestor of Boccaccio's and Chaucer's Criseyde), Benoit gives the story its medieval form, making a coherent narrative out of the earlier versions, developing the important characters, and weaving in dramatic material from important classical and medieval sources. His version, in turn, was translated into Latin prose by the Italian writer Guido delle Colonne in his *Historia Destructionis Troiae* (1287).[9] Without acknowledging his debt to Benoit, Guido reworks the story as a history, retaining Benoit's embellishments, but abridging some of the descriptions and adding several moral and philosophical digressions. For Guido, the Troy narrative is important not as an exciting story, but primarily as a serious history that could benefit later generations, and it is this emphasis that the late medieval authors of the Troy story—the writer of the *Alliterative Destruction of Troy*, the *Laud Troy Book*, and Lydgate—admire. While Chaucer and Boccaccio develop the love story of Troilus and Criseyde, these writers renew the effort to encompass in a single work the complete history of Troy from the expedition of the Argonauts to the destruction of all of the Trojan heroes. Although their purposes in retelling the story differ, each writer further amplifies the legend which, along with the destruction of King Arthur's court and the fall of Alexander, dominates the late medieval narrative vision.

The "Trouthe" of the Story: Guido and Lydgate

In his prologue to the *Troy Book*, Lydgate sets up Guido as the model among the various authorities for the story of Troy, for he best represents the two goals Lydgate announces for himself at the outset—truthfulness and eloquent style. Diverging considerably from the prologue of the *Historia*, Lydgate establishes these ideals, which he links together, as the basis for the poet's reworking of the past. As he reminds his reader, good poets work to direct the audience's attention to the underlying truth of their sources, thereby preserving valuable sentence from destruction:

> For in her honde they hilde for a staf
> The trouthe only, whyche thei han compyled
> Vn-to this fyn, that we wer nat begyled
> Of necligence thoruȝ forȝetfilnesse.
> (prologue, ll. 152–55)

The poet's eloquence illuminates old stories so that man may comprehend their "sentence." Lydgate explains that skillful writers "Han trewly set thoruȝ diligent labour, / And enlumyned with many corious flour / Of rethorik, to make vs comprehende / The trouthe of al, as it was in kende . . ." (prologue ll. 217–20). Thus, Lydgate concludes his prologue by praising Guido's skill in illuminating the Troy legend by his rhetoric (prologue, ll. 361–67).

In amplifying Guido's brief prologue to introduce these concerns, Lydgate establishes his responsibility as poet to the past. While Chaucer questions the relation of the poet to the events of history in his version of the Troy story, he avoids resolving the dilemma inherent in the poet-historian's effort—the conflict between his desire to provide a truthful vision and his awareness of the limitations of his human medium.[10] With several skillful ploys, Chaucer underscores the problems mortal man confronts as artist and concludes with a lingering uncertainty about the poet's ability to embody firm truths in his fictions. Lydgate, in contrast, begins with the assurance that the poet's effort leads man to truth.

In restructuring Guido's account, Lydgate indicates he attempts to preserve its sentence in English, "As in latyn and in frensche it is; / That of the story þe trouth[e] we nat mys / No more than doth eche other nacioun . . ." (prologue, ll. 115–17). In translating, he makes a considerable number of changes, expanding the Latin prose version to nearly 30,000 lines. The overall design of his additions is purposeful, although at times the thematic emphasis Lydgate introduces is blurred by his digressions. In contrast to Guido, who organizes his material in thirty-five short books, Lydgate reworks the narrative into five distinct units designed structurally to emphasize the theme of the loss which results from war. Each of the five sections ends with a climactic event that points up this theme. Book 1, which describes the expedition of the Argonauts and Jason's reign as king of Thessaly, concludes with the total destruction of Old Troy. Book 2, which begins with the building of the splendid city of New Troy, ultimately reveals the feuds and disorder produced by Helen's abduction, and ends with the Greek soldiers ominously encamped outside the city, threatening all that Priam and his followers have created. After a long series of battles between the two armies, book 3 closes with the tragic death of Hector, the greatest of the Trojan heroes. Book 4, in many ways the most splendid, concludes with the total destruction of New Troy while the final book closes the epic with the death of all the heroes, the flower of Greek and Trojan chivalry.

The view of the fall of Troy as an example of the irreparable loss of war is reinforced by Lydgate's major categories of additions—comments on the dangers of war, on the ways in which small sparks or slight causes grow into great fires, and on the vicissitudes of Fortune. In a long digression at the outset of book 1, Lydgate introduces these themes. Old Troy, he suggests, was destroyed by Fortune "for no þing but þat Fortune wolde / Schewen her mȝgt and her cruelte, / In vengaunce takyng vp-on þis cite" (*TB,* 1.776–78). The Trojans in the heat of their anger did not see that a small spark if not extinguished would level the entire city. As Lydgate laments:

> Allas, þat euere so worþi of estate
> Schulde for lytel fallen at debate!
> Whan it is gonne it is not lyȝt to staunche:
> For of griffyng of a lytel braunche,
> Ful sturdy trees growe[n] vp ful ofte;
> Who clymbeth hyȝe may not falle softe;
> And of sparkys þat ben of syȝt[e] smale,
> Is fire engendered þat devoureth al. . . .
> (*TB,* 1.779–86)

The end of this "lytel" fire, Lydgate warns, is death and destruction for all. The same emphasis is found in several of the additions throughout the poem, most notably in the long digression about Fortune at the outset of book 2, the scathing rebuke of Priam for seeking vengeance against the Greeks, in the dramatic speeches of Hector and Agamemnon against war, in the narrator's repeated laments for the needless destruction of Greek and Trojan chivalry, and in the splendid prologue to book 4 against Mars, the hateful God of war.[11]

Lydgate further refines the moral emphasis of his source in the lengthy passages he inserts about the relation of men and Fortune. Although he begins in book 1 with the familiar stance found in Guido that Fortune is a lady of "transmvtacioun," false and unstable, who leads fools to harm (*TB,* 1.2258 ff.), he gradually modifies this view to link Fortune's power with man's moral character. Diverging from Guido, he suggests that man has means to safeguard himself against Fortune by his prudence and wisdom, for Fortune controls only the weak and unwise. The narrator thus berates Medea for not anticipating Jason's falseness (*TB,* 1.3599 ff.), chides Lamedon for trusting in her gifts (*TB,* 1.69 ff.), and complains about Priam's indiscretion and haste in fighting the Greeks (*TB,* 1.1797 ff.). Echoing Boethius, Lydgate suggests that disaster comes to these men and women not by chance, but because they foolishly choose to submit themselves to her power. Finally, in some passages which he adds to Guido, Lydgate links Fortune with divine justice, indicating that men get the Fortune they deserve. In book 4, for example, after cataloging the injuries that Fortune has done to the Greeks, Agamemnon, in a passage Lydgate adds to his source, argues that the Greeks have the power to buffet themselves against these harms (*TB,* 4.3278–84). Similarly, in book 5, Lydgate moves from the essentially Boethian argument that man must not put his faith in the false goods of the world to the notion that men have some control over their own Fortune and that Fortune is just and subject to God's will (*TB,* 5.3576–86).

A Mirror for Kings

In books 2 and 3, Lydgate begins to develop his material more explicitly as a king's mirror, linking his thematic concerns with the dangers of war and the workings of Fortune with the actions of the individual heroes. Reworking Guido, he treats the major characters in these books—Hector, Paris, Achilles, and Troilus—as exemplary types of behavior to imitate or avoid as a leader. While Paris, Achilles, and Troilus are led astray by passion and jeopardize the fate of their companions, Hector, though vulnerable to human temptations, remains dedicated to the ideals of the true chivalric hero which Lydgate associates in his prologue with Henry V. At the outset of book 2, Lydgate expands Guido's one-sentence description to introduce Hector as the epitome of knightly qualities whose renown and worthiness are known throughout the realm:

> . . . liche as bokis of hym specefye,
> He was the Rote and stok of cheualrie,
> And of knyȝthod verray souereyn flour,
> þe sowrs and welle of worschip & honour;
> And of manhod, I dar it wel expresse,
> Example and merour; & of hiȝe prowesse,
> Gynyng & grounde; & with al þis I-fere,

> Wonder benigne & lawly of his chere,
> Discret also, prudent and vertuous.
> (*TB*, 2.243–51)

Similarly, in the council scene, he amplifies Guido's account to emphasize Hector's gentility and courtesy (*TB*, 2.2179–80). Although Lydgate follows Guido's outline for Hector's speech, he adds a long digression which draws attention to the exemplary value of Hector's views against war. Interrupting the narrative before the council scene, Lydgate berates Priam for his rash decision to fight the Greeks, warning him of the recklessness of Fortune and of the danger of beginning a war without anticipating its ending. In Lydgate's version, Hector echoes these words, urging Priam to consider the outcome before initiating a war (*TB*, 2.2229–54). In addition to being prudent, Hector is the model of human valor, the worthiest and boldest of men. Again amplifying Guido's account, Lydgate underscores these qualities in the battle scenes at the end of book 2 and the beginning of book 3 (*TB*, 2.8468 ff.; 3.480 ff., 841 ff., 1107 ff.).

But it is in presenting the death of Hector that Lydgate deviates most significantly from Guido's treatment by giving Hector a human flaw which precipitates his downfall. Although Hector is warned by Andromache, Cassandra, and Priam not to fight, in both versions he rushes out to battle, enraged by the news of Margarytone's death. In Guido's account, after many intense encounters, Hector finally is killed by Achilles who catches him unprotected with his shield on his back as he attempts to drag a Greek king away from the troops. Guido implies that without taking this unfair advantage of Hector, Achilles might not have been able to defeat him.[12] Lydgate considerably changes Guido's emphasis. He first builds up the importance of Hector as a Trojan warrior and the threat he represents to the Greek forces. He then expands the final encounter between Hector and Achilles, making Hector more clearly responsible for his own death. In Lydgate's version, Hector covets the splendid armor of one of the slain Greek kings and is in the process of stripping the corpse when Achilles overcomes him. As Lydgate laments, his covetousness momentarily mars his knightly perfection and brings about his ruin:

> . . . allas! on fals couetyse!
> Whos gredy fret,—þe which is gret pite,—

In hertis may nat liȝtly staunchid be;
þe etyk gnaweþ be so gret distresse,
þat it diffaceth þe hiȝe conquerours,
And of her fame rent aweie þe flours.
Desyre of hauynge, in a gredy þouȝt,
To hiȝe noblesse sothly longeth nouȝt,
No[r] swiche pelfre, spoillynge, nor robberie
Apartene to worþi chiualrye. . . .
(*TB*, 3.5353–62)

After Hector's death, Lydgate again adds a long rhetorical passage in which he prays for help from the various muses to deal adequately with the loss of this hero, the worthiest of men (*TB*, 3.5480–94). Lydgate's changes thus establish Hector as an exemplary, yet human, figure, a model for imitation, yet a reminder of the need for moral vigilance. He is at once a type of the chivalric knight Henry V admires and an example of the struggle required to attain this ideal.

In contrast, Lydgate treats the characters of Paris, Achilles, and to some extent Troilus, as foils for Hector. Each of these characters in Lydgate's version subjects the ideals of the chivalric hero to a passion that is potentially dangerous and destructive. Paris' desire for Helen leads to the outbreak of the war and the eventual fall of Troy. Considerably amplifying Paris' speech and his account of his encounter with Venus, Minerva, and Juno, Lydgate emphasizes the allegorical significance of the goddesses and the implications of Paris' choice of Venus, the goddess of love. While Guido merely reports the episode in fifty-eight lines, Lydgate develops the scene as a full-fledged allegory of man's choices of passion, wisdom, and fortune.[13] Similarly, Lydgate represents Troilus, who has the reputation of being "Hector þe secounde / For his manhood" (*TB*, 2.288–89) as momentarily distracted by his passion for Criseyde and in danger of being blinded to the appropriate course of action for the Trojans. But while Paris' love leads to the downfall of the Trojans, Troilus finally subjects his passion to the larger cause, and his love leads not to the destruction of the city but to his own death at the hands of his rival Diomede. Finally, in book 4, Lydgate emphasizes that Achilles' desire for Polexyna prevents him from fulfilling his role as a Greek champion as he takes to his tent sick for love. Urging the Greeks to make peace against their best interests, he subjects the concerns of the country to his personal desire.

"In englysche to translate"

Despite the recurrent emphasis on the dangers of war, the workings of Fortune, and the activity appropriate to the wise and prudent hero, these themes do not appear to have been Lydgate's major concern in reworking Guido's narrative. As critics have pointed out, in addition to these passages, Lydgate inserts many apparently extraneous lines—seasonal introductions, elaborate descriptions, set speeches, lengthy laments and invectives, and eloquent sections of narrative comment and digressions.[14] These additions reveal Lydgate's concern with elevating the narrative, with creating a work in English that is loftier and more impressive than any before him. Together, these passages comprise about one third of the poem and create a version of the Troy story that differs substantially in its impact from the earlier medieval accounts.

The effect of Lydgate's experimentation is immediately apparent in turning to the *Troy Book* from Guido's *Historia*. As Lydgate translates, he transforms the brief descriptions in these accounts into skillful passages of extended commentary. Book 1 is typical of his treatment. The book begins with the story of Peleus' attempt to have his nephew Jason killed by sending him on the expedition to win the Golden Fleece. But after eight lines of narrative, Lydgate amplifies Guido's Ovidian digression about the Myrmidons before resuming the story some 84 lines later. Following Guido, he narrates the account of Peleus' rivalry with Aeson, adding a rhetorical digression about the sin of covetousness which prompts Peleus' wicked behavior. Continuing the story, he describes the building and outfitting of the Argon, the warriors who join Jason, including Hercules for whom Lydgate pauses to insert a digression about his twelve labors. Before returning to Guido's narrative, he adds an elaborate astrological description and then inserts into the account of the Greek expedition a lengthy reminder of the ways in which slight causes grow into significant wars. Lydgate and Guido both report the landing of the Argonauts near Troy, their expulsion by Lamedon, their arrival at Colchos, and the winning of the Golden Fleece with Medea's help. But Lydgate seizes every opportunity to amplify Guido's matter, routinely expanding the characters' speeches, the descriptive passages about the places the Greeks land, and the appearance and traits of the characters.

A typical example of his changes is provided by his treatment of the Trojans' arrival at the island of Colchos and the city of Jacontis at the beginning of the book.[15] By his rhetorical amplification, Lydgate turns Guido's fifteen-line passage into 147 lines of elegant description. He first prefaces his version with an elaborate account of daybreak (*TB,* 1.11979–1214). Then, following Guido, he represents Jason and his men aboard their ships en route to Colchos where they will land at the splendid city of Jachonitos. But while Guido merely remarks that this city was established as the capital of the kingdom on account of its size and was "an extremely beautiful city surrounded by walls and towers, embellished with many skillfully constructed palaces, filled with a large populace, and distinguished by being the home of many noblemen,"[16] Lydgate provides a magnificent description of an earthly paradise. The city itself in Lydgate's version is stately and impressive: "With stretes large and corious howsyng. . . . Strong[e] wallid & toured rounde aboute, / Of huge heiȝte and aboue batailled, / Maskued also, lyst þei wer assailed, / With many palys, staatly and royal . . ." (1.1252–55). Around the city are bountiful rivers, plains, parks, and woods teeming with life and color which Lydgate celebrates in more than forty lines of extended praise (1.1265–1309).

The central episode of book 1, the love story of Jason and Medea, grows in Lydgate's treatment from 247 lines in Guido to more than 2,100 lines, embellished by outbursts on the beauty and learning of Medea, on the powers of God compared to the powers of Medea, on the unfairness of Guido in denigrating women, on the growing love of Jason and Medea, on the duplicity of Jason, and on the misery of Medea.[17] The book ends with the siege and destruction of Old Troy.

In a similar fashion, Lydgate expands book 2 with digressions on idolatry, descriptions of the Greek and Trojan warriors, comments on the origins of chess (ll. 816 ff.) and the performance of plays (ll. 860 ff.), and moralizing outbursts against Fortune (ll. 2018 ff.), women, gambling, and drink, and passages of political advice. In book 3, he considerably heightens and intensifies the action by adding a long emotionalized lament at the parting of Troilus and Criseyde (ll. 4077 ff.), focusing on the lovers' sorrow and despair. Many of these interpolated passages, particularly the digressions about women and Fortune, were anthologized by Lydgate's contemporaries, who responded to the poem as a series of topics or exempla for amplification.[18]

Lydgate, however, is most successful in his effort to extend the scale and scope of his story in book 4, the section which deals with the final battles and destruction of Troy. In this portion of the poem, he brings his two concerns together most effectively, exploiting his grandiose and elevated version of Guido's narrative to underscore the magnitude of the loss, the inevitable futility of war. Book 4 stands out from the rest of the narrative in a number of ways. The book is proportionally longer than the others in relation to its source and is characterized by a greater number of additions which function to elevate the action. In this book, Lydgate uses several devices to extend his material. Most obviously, he punctuates the events with a series of eloquent set speeches, more than twenty major speeches in this book alone. The section opens with a magnificent address of Agamemnon adapted from a rather brief and colorless passage in Guido (4.11–103), and, as the book unfolds, the eloquence and intensity of the speeches increases, reinforcing the mounting intensity of the action. The next speech, Achilles' address to the Greeks, is even longer and more elaborate than Agamemnon's (4.960–1134). Expanding twenty-five lines of his source into 174 lines of highly charged invective, Lydgate creates a climactic moment of suspended commentary on the action in which Achilles bids his audience take heed of all they jeopardize by coming to Troy. Dramatically, he points to his own wounds and loss of blood and demands, with heightened rhetoric, whether Helen is worth such a price.

The tendencies apparent in Achilles' outburst increase in the next two speeches, the interchange between Ulysses and Achilles.[19] In these passages, Lydgate turns Guido's series of rhetorical questions into two lofty and impassioned addresses which raise a major crux in the poem. Ulysses, on the one hand, cautiously addresses Achilles, points to the change in his words, and reminds him of the terrible consequences that will ensue if he does not fight. Upbraiding him for ignoring the opportunity Fortune provides, he concludes with a highly charged outburst against sloth (*TB,* 4.1790–1803). Achilles responds "for anger ded and pale" (l. 1808) in a masterful revision of Guido's lines. With hammerlike strokes of rhetoric, he reminds Ulysses that they risk all of Greek chivalry, perhaps all of the gentle blood of Greece, for a paltry thing. He will not jeopardize his life any further for fame which is "but a wynde" (*TB,* 4.1872–80).

The series of speeches in book 4 is climaxed by the most elaborate and emotional of all as Hecuba reproaches Aeneas for his betrayal of Troy. Priam has been murdered; Troy lies in ashes, and as Hecuba and Polyxena flee, they stumble upon the traitor Aeneas. Hecuba musters her last measure of strength and dignity to upbraid him in a magnificent passage Lydgate transforms from Guido's account:

> O þou traitour, most malicious!
> þou false serpent, adder envious!
> Crop and rote, fynder of falsnesse,
> Sours and well of vnkyndnesse,
> How myȝtestow in þin herte fynde
> Vn-to þi kyng to be so vnkynde?—
> Gynner and ground, exaumple of tresoun,
> And final cause of oure destruccioun!
> How myȝt[e]stow, devoide of al pite,
> Be hold, allas! þoruȝ þi cruelte
> Of þi kyng to shede so þe blood,
> þat euere haþ ben so gentil & so good,
> So graceous lord, specialy to the!
> (*TB,* 4.6441–53)

She then abruptly changes her tone in the second half of the speech and delivers an emotional plea to Aeneas to pity Polyxena, summing up the mood of anger and loss which characterize this section.[20]

Lydgate reinforces the effect created by these speeches by several other categories of additions—seasonal prefaces, elaborate descriptive passages, eloquent sections of narrative comment. But his efforts to elevate the Troy narrative are most striking in the series of laments that culminate in this section of the poem. While this type of addition punctuates the entire work, it is introduced with marked frequency in book 4, producing a striking specter of past grandeur and immediate loss. Lydgate first sounds this note in his description of Hector's funeral and Hecuba's and Polyxena's grief (*TB,* 4.518 ff.). Against the backdrop of the Greeks' celebration, he represents the stately procession of the Trojans and the piercing cries of the women. The sense of loss builds as Lydgate introduces in rapid succession outbursts on the death of Troilus (4.2668 ff., 2998 ff.), Achilles (4.3210 ff.), and Paris (4.3616 ff.), and finally caps this series with an eloquent address to Mars, a passage that is even more rhetorical and ornate than the preceding laments:

> O cruel Mars, þat hast made for to fyne
> þoruȝ þin Ire al þe worþi blood
> Of Troie, allas! why hastow ben so wood
> Ageyn[e]s hem, to slen her knyȝtes alle?
> Why hastow lete þi bitter venym falle
> On hem, allas, þou sterre infortunat!—
> With al þe world to make hem at debat,
> O hatful sterre, hoot, combust, and drye,
> Fyry, Irous, grounde of al envie,
> Hasty euere, ful of discencioun. . . .
> (*TB*, 4.4440–49)

Five more laments follow for the deeds of the various traitors against Troy.[21] Finally, book 4 ends with the most ambitious lament of all, Lydgate's six-page farewell to the fallen Troy, an impressive passage for which there is no hint in his source (*TB*, 4.6932–7102).

The effect Lydgate finally produces by his manipulation of the Troy narrative differs from Guido's. Lydgate's changes in the *Troy Book* reveal his concern with elevating the narrative and creating a monumental version of the story in English, loftier and more impressive than any before him. In the numerous digressions about writing which he adds to his source, he particularly emphasizes the importance of his efforts as a poet working in English. At the outset of the prologue, he indicates that he attempts a version of the story in English equal to the Latin and French narratives so that its fame will survive "In oure tonge, aboute in euery age" (prologue, l. 113). In his repeated praise of Chaucer, Lydgate develops these concerns by singling out Chaucer's achievement as an English poet who first made his native tongue worthy of significant poetry:

> Noble Galfride, poete of Breteyne,
> Amonge oure englisch þat made first to reyne
> þe gold dewe-dropis of rethorik so fyne,
> Oure rude langage only tenlwmyne.
> (*TB*, 2.4697–4700)

Before Chaucer, English was "rude and boistous" and incapable of ambitious literary efforts. Chaucer refined and adorned our native speech, and, in effect, put English on the map as a poetic language:

For he owre englishe gilt[e] with hys sawes,
Rude and boistous firste be olde dawes,
þat was ful fer from al perfeccioun,
And but of litel reputacioun,
Til þat he cam, &, þoruȝ his poetrie,
Gan oure tonge firste to magnifie,
And adourne it with his elloquence. . . .
(*TB,* 3.4237–43)

It is in this effort to extend the limits of his medium as an English poet that Lydgate seeks to emulate Chaucer in the *Troy Book.* Although his attempt is not always successful—the action at times becomes tedious, particularly near the end of the poem—Lydgate's experiment in this work introduces themes and strategies that will be more effectively handled in his next two long poems, the *Siege of Thebes* and the *Fall of Princes.*

The Poet as Civilizer

Although the stories of Troy and Thebes frequently appear together in manuscripts of the fourteenth and fifteenth centuries and were associated in style and purpose, Lydgate's versions differ conspicuously from each other.[22] The *Siege of Thebes* is brief by Lydgatian standards, a mere 4,716 lines as opposed to the more than 29,700 lines of the *Troy Book.* Most of the features characteristic of Lydgate's style in the *Troy Book*—the rhetorical amplification, eloquent outbursts, elaborately extended descriptions, and elevated digressions—occur only rarely or are notably absent from this work. In the *Siege,* Lydgate follows his sources—a late French prose version of the *Roman de Thebes* and Boccaccio's *De genealogia deorum* and *De claris mulieribus*—with much greater freedom than he does in the *Troy Book.* Despite his repeated insistence that he has been brief,[23] he adds more than 1,570 lines, or about one third of the poem, to his source. But in contrast to the *Troy Book,* with few exceptions, the interpolations in the *Siege of Thebes* are didactic and serve to reinforce the central theme of the poem. Without sacrificing the scale of the poem, in the *Siege* Lydgate creates a structure in which the emphasis is squarely on the moral significance of the story. Working on his own initiative without the aid of a patron, a procedure that is rare for him, Lydgate pursues concerns that he treated only inchoately in the *Troy Book* to develop this poem explicitly as a king's mirror.

At the outset of the *Siege of Thebes,* Lydgate underscores this emphasis by his exploitation of the myth of Amphion, the legendary founder of the city. Departing from his source in book 1, he introduces a lengthy account of Amphion's founding of Thebes, drawn primarily from Boccaccio's *De genealogia deorum.*[24] As he explains, Amphion built the walls of Thebes only with "the swetnesse / and melodious soun // And armonye / of his swete song . . ." (*ST,* ll. 202–3), for he had a unique power of eloquence that he received from Mercury at birth. Adding to Boccaccio's version, Lydgate links Amphion's "song" with his "crafty speech" and "his wordes swete" that were so "pleasaunt," "favorable," and "mete" that they caused all to do his bidding in concord: "In her Eerys / that shortly was ther noon // Disobeysaunt / with the kyng to goon, // Wher so euere / that hym list assigne" (*ST,* ll. 231–33). Again departing from Boccaccio, Lydgate draws the following moral from the story of Amphion: the "ssote sugred harpe" of Mercury is more fortunate than the sword of Mars. A ruler can achieve more by eloquent words than by force:

> I take record / of Kyng Amphyoun,
> That bylte Thebes be his elloquence
> Mor than of Pride / or of violence,
> Noble and riche / that lik was nowher non,
> And thus the walles / mad of lym and stoon
> Were reised first / be syngyng of this kyng. . . .
> (*ST,* ll. 286–91)

By his manipulation of the story of Amphion, Lydgate introduces a major theme in the *Siege of Thebes*—the opposition of the word and the sword. Restructuring his material, he develops the entire poem as an example of this concern. By means of his additions, which cluster at six or seven critical points in the narrative—in the encounters between Adrastus, Tydeus, and Polyneices, and Tydeus and Eteocles, and in the passages relating to Hypsipyle, in the scenes between Jocasta and Polyneices, in the final battle between Eteocles and Polyneices, and in the lengthy epilogue which he adds to the poem—Lydgate develops a series of incidents that exemplify the oppositions of the opening description of Amphion. Part 1 provides the background to the conflict with its account of two contrasting types of rulers, Amphion and Oedipus, whose actions lead to the founding and the destruction of Thebes.

In parts 2 and 3, Lydgate structures several episodes to illustrate the successful triumph of words over the sword. At the outset of book 2, for example, when the two knights, Tydeus and Polyneices, first meet at night in a storm, their impulse is to fight to see who will win the right to stay in the shelter. Their quarrel awakens Adrastus, the king of Argos, who, like Amphion, persuades them by his eloquent words to put aside their swords. This decision proves fortuitous for both men, for Adrastus befriends them, marries them to his daughters, and gives each of them riches and half a kingdom.[25] An even more dramatic example occurs in book 3 when the Greeks are aided by Lady Hypsipyle.[26] Desperately in need of water, the Greeks enter a garden where they find the lady caring for a child, the son of King Lycurgus. After hearing Tydeus' plea, Hypsipyle promises to fetch water for the weary men. But while she is gone, a serpent poisons the child who is sleeping in the garden and he instantly dies. At first, the queen urges Lycurgus to seek revenge with his sword, but ultimately he is persuaded by Adrastus' "sweet words" to forgive Hypsipyle and avoid war.

In contrast to these examples, Lydgate develops a number of incidents to emphasize the disastrous consequences that ensue when the sword is allowed to gain precedent over the word. The first example involves Tydeus' embassy to Thebes to persuade Eteocles to fulfill his promise to Polyneices to turn the kingdom over to him for a year.[27] Tydeus speaks courteously and eloquently, but Eteocles ignores his arguments. The result is the beginning of the war of Thebes in which both kingdoms are destroyed. Similarly, during the wars the prophet Amphiorax tries to persuade the Greeks to give up their siege.[28] But the Greeks spurn his language and their effort ends in disaster. Finally, in an episode that directly parallels the incident in which Tydeus acts as a messenger to Eteocles, Jocasta journeys to Thebes to persuade her son, Eteocles, to become reconciled with Polyneices and end the war.[29] Lydgate amplifies the description of the Greeks encamped around Thebes and the perilous position of the Thebans. Surrounded by enemies, Eteocles takes council to determine whether to fight or yield. Again, Lydgate adds to his source the climactic speech of Jocasta which reiterates the sentence of the opening example of Amphion—it is better to put one's trust in honorable words than in the sword:

> . . . it is foly / be short avisement,
> To putte a strif / in martys Iugement.
> For hard it is / whan a Iuge is wood,
> To tret aforn hym / with-out loss of blood.
> And ȝif we put our mater / hool in Marte,
> which with the swerd / his lawes doth coarte,
> Than may hit happe / when ȝe be glad or loth,
> Thow and thy brother / shal repente both;
> And many a-noþer / that is her present,
> Of ȝoure trespas / than ben Innocent. . . .
> (*ST,* ll. 3661–70)

Eteocles disregards her advice and brings disaster and suffering to all. As Lydgate points out, this is the inevitable result when war wins over words, when the sword of Mars is favored more than the harp of Mercury. The poem ends with the hope that war will cease and love and peace will spread:

> . . . Martys swerd / shal no more manace,
> Nor his spere / greuous to sustene,
> Shal now no more / whettyd be so kene,
> Nor he no more / shal his hauberk shake.
> But loue and pees / in hertys shal awake,
> And charite, / both in length and brede,
> Of newee shal her bryghte beemys sprede
> Thorgh grace / only in dyuers naciouns,
> Forto reforme / a-twixe Regyouns
> Pees and quyet / concord and vnyte.
> (*ST,* ll. 4694–4703)

These words echo the language of the recently concluded Treaty of Troyes (1420) which was to lead to the union of England and France and the end of the Hundred Years War through the marriage of King Henry V of England and Katherine of France.[30] But the intent of the treaty and the desire for peace was to be undermined by the death of Henry V in 1422.

An Example for Rulers

In delineating the various characters in the poem, Lydgate reshapes the Thebes story explicitly as a mirror for kings.[31] Developing themes briefly introduced in the *Troy Book,* he treats the major figures—Amphion, Eteocles, Polyneices, Adrastus, and Tydeus—as types of the good and bad ruler. The figure of Amphion in part 1 provides the model of the just king who wins his subjects' support by his prudence, kindness, goodness, and love:

> For a humble speche / wiþ glad contenaunce
> May a prynce / sothly more avaunce
> Among his puple / Hertes forto wynne
> Of inward loue / which that wol not twynne,
> Than gold / rychesse / pride / or tyranye,
> Outher disdeyne / daunger / or surqueyde.
> (*ST,* ll. 277–82)

Similarly, Adrastus earns the loyalty of Polyneices and Tydeus by his generosity and kindness.

In contrast to these rulers is the tyrant Eteocles, who defies the ideals of the just king. Adding considerably to his source, Lydgate presents Eteocles as the betrayer of truth, the virtue which is the preserver of the kingdom and its prosperity and above all others must be revered by the king: "abouen alle thyng // Trouthe shulde / longe to a kyng, // Of his word / not be variable, // But pleyn / and hool / as a Centre stable. // For trouthe first / with-outen eny wene, // Is Chief Pyler / that may a kyng sustene . . ." (*ST,* ll. 1721–26). In violating this ideal by his falseness, Eteocles brings about the ruin of Thebes. In part 3, Lydgate stresses the similar importance of love for a king. Expanding his source, he argues that love is more effective than gold in winning the people over to a king, for "Gold faileth ofte / loue wol abyde // For lyf or deth / be a lordys syde; // And the tresour / shortly, of a kyng // Stondeth in loue / abouen alle thyng . . ." (*ST,* 3.2716–20). Eteocles, who turns his back on love to choose war, ignores the responsibility of the king. As Jocasta warns him in a speech which Lydgate adds to his source, it is folly to reject love and turn to Mars' judgment (*ST,* ll. 3661–69).

Finally, in his treatment of the character of Tydeus, Lydgate brings together all of the qualities of the perfect knight. Like Amphion and Adrastus, he works for peace rather than war, acting as emissary to Eteocles to dissuade him from his misguided course of action. Loyal to his lord, he is unusually brave in battle and the model of the courtly knight with women. In fighting the Thebans, for example, he defends himself single-handedly against fifty men, winning the battle (*ST,* ll. 2133 ff.). He is courteous to Lycurgus' daughter who nurses him back to health after this battle, but he takes no advantage of her favors, choosing to return to his land and the service of his lord. Temperate and prudent in his views, he provides the counterpart to the rash actions of Eteocles. In the final battle, for example, Tydeus avoids entering Thebes in haste and risking the lives of his men (*ST,* ll. 3972 ff.). In short, Lydgate emphasizes, he was "The beste knyght / and most manly man" (*ST,* ll. 4231).

Lydgate draws attention to his strategy of developing the *Siege of Thebes* as a king's mirror by placing his effort in the context of an issue that had received repeated emphasis in Chaucer's *Canterbury Tales,* that of telling a beneficial or useful tale. In the frames to several of the *Canterbury Tales,* Chaucer links this problem with his changing definition of the term "myrie tale."[32] The Host consistently assigns one meaning to this phrase—a tale that entertains or amuses, a "murie thyng of aventures."[33]

In contrast to the Host's definition, as the work unfolds Chaucer develops another definition of the "myrie tale" that includes three overtly didactic tales—the *Melibee,* an allegory; the *Nun's Priest's Tale,* a fable; and the *Parson's Tale,* a sermon. In the frames to these tales, he introduces the term to redress the balance between performance and sentence, between the effort to entertain the audience and the effort to instruct it. Ultimately, in the introduction to the *Parson's Tale,* he links the "myrie tale" with the notion of a "fructuous" or beneficial tale, indicating in this last definition that a "myrie tale" is one which effectively combines sentence and solace to point up the moral significance of the text, a tale that clears up the reader's perception and teaches him to "understonde." But, ironically, in order to produce this kind of tale and avoid the ambiguities of language and theme that many of the other tales raise, Chaucer finds it necessary to abandon fiction. The *Parson's Tale,* his concluding tale, significantly is the only one of the *Canterbury Tales* which is not a story. Chaucer thus leaves us with an imperfect solution. In raising the issue of a "myrie tale," he examines the criteria of a good tale, but at the same time he makes us poignantly aware of the limits of man's art to achieve them.

In the prologue to the *Siege of Thebes,* Lydgate returns to the issue of a "myrie tale." Explicitly framing his poem as a "Canterbury Tale," he recalls the context of the Host's discussion in Chaucer's work. When Lydgate enters the inn, for example, the Host makes much of his dreary appearance as a monk (prologue, ll. 83–90). Echoing his earlier speeches in the *Canterbury Tales,* he challenges Daun John, despite his dull appearance, to tell a tale of mirth or gladness:

> Tel some tale / and make ther-of a Iape!
> For be my Rouncy / thow shalt not eskape.
> But preche not / of non holynesse!
> Gynne some tale / of myrth or of gladnesse,
> And nodde not / with thyn heuy bekke!
> Telle vs some thyng / that draweþ to effecte
> Only of Ioye! / make no longer lette!
> (prologue, ll. 165–71)

Lydgate's response is a tale that satisfies Chaucer's larger definition of a "myrie tale" rather than the Host's and, at the same time, qualifies it. Like Chaucer, he attempts to tell a tale which is "myrie" in a larger sense than the Host requested, that is, one that is not simply entertaining, but fruitful or beneficial to its audience. But Lydgate introduces the possibility of a "fructuous" tale which is not developed in the *Canterbury Tales*—the moral speculum or tale which is beneficial practically rather than spiritually. His "Canterbury Tale" substitutes for the explicit moral forms, the allegory, the fable, and the sermon, a familiar narrative that he turns into a mirror of political "moralitee." In contrast to Chaucer's concern about the ambiguity of poetry, Lydgate's transformation of the "myrie tale" reveals his confidence in the power of poetry to order and to civilize men. His "Canterbury Tale," finally, is not a clumsy imitation of Chaucer's work as critics have suggested, but an attempt to deal with an issue Chaucer raises and resolves in one way in his poems.

Lydgate's experimentation in the *Troy Book* and the *Siege of Thebes* reveals his effort to direct his craft as poet to the well-being of the state. Reworking these two familiar stories, he underscores the political relevance of the past to the present situation, at first tentatively and intermittently in the *Troy Book* and then more explicitly in the *Siege of Thebes.* Linking the poet's eloquence with wisdom, virtue, and order he suggests that, like the legendary king, Amphion, the poet is a civilizer of men. In this role, he is poignantly aware of his responsibility as an English poet, who, like his master, Chaucer, works within a literary medium that is in the process of attaining a new importance and stature. In both the *Troy Book* and the *Siege of Thebes,* Lydgate addresses poetic issues Chaucer introduces in his *Troilus* and *Canterbury Tales*—the relation of the poet to the matter of the past, the possibility of creating works of significant scale and scope in the changing and imperfect vernacular, and the definition of a "myrie" or effective tale. But although he responds to Chaucer's concerns, Lydgate undertakes solutions that finally move the long form in different directions than Chaucer's—toward a conspicuously amplified and elevated narrative in the *Troy Book,* greater in scale than any English poem before it and toward the king's mirror or political exemplum in the *Siege of Thebes.* In these two related stories, Lydgate establishes himself as an English poet of importance and as a poet concerned with order in the world rather than the transcendental journeys of Dante, Langland, and Chaucer.

Chapter Four

The *Fall of Princes:* Fortune and the Lives of Men

In the *Fall of Princes,* Lydgate engages in his most ambitious experimentation with the long form in English. A work of more than 36,000 lines, the poem occupied his attention, with brief pauses for other short commissions, during the period between 1431 and 1438–39. Beginning with the fall of Adam and Eve, the poem surveys all known history, classical, biblical, and medieval, up to the reign of King John of France. Developing the concerns of the king's mirror that he had introduced in the *Troy Book* and the *Siege of Thebes,* Lydgate, like his predecessors Boccaccio and Laurent de Premierfait, culls the remains of ancient myth and modern legend to assemble examples of the rise and fall of great men. In his sweeping vision, Troy and Thebes become but two episodes in a larger pattern of human activity. Lydgate's focus shifts from historical narrative to the underlying order or design in the lives of men. Two forces particularly—the unsettling operation of Fortuna and individual moral choices—come under his scrutiny as determinants of man's fate, and Lydgate considers with interest the moments when these forces clash. But in the vast panorama of history, all human order, however sound, finally appears transitory, and Lydgate manipulates the expansive form of his poem to underscore this theme. As poet, he indicates, his role is to contend with the destructive power of Fortuna by providing models of the civilizing and ordering abilities of men.

The Tradition of the Fall of Princes

The account of the fall of great men has fascinated audiences for centuries. The most powerful of the Greek tragedies—*Oedipus Rex, Oedipus at Colonus, Medea,* and *Hippolytus* among others—center around the fatal flaw or imperceivable error that changes the fate of strong and impressive men and women. This situation, Aristotle suggests, is capable of arousing in the audience "pity and fear" which accomplish a "catharsis of emotions."[1] In Roman times, the Greek biographer, Plutarch (46–120 A.D.), who lectured and traveled in Rome, wrote a series of forty-six *Parallel Lives* that report the careers, successes, and reversals of noted statesmen. Frequently pairing Greek and Roman figures, Plutarch underscores the ethical basis for their sudden and similar turns of fate. These stories impressed medieval readers who had access to them in compilations of tragedies and moralized collections. In the early Middle Ages, the interest in the lives of great men surfaced in the numerous histories of the emerging empires, for example, the narratives of Charlemagne and Saint Louis in France.[2] In England, these accounts are especially prominent in the works of the Anglo-Norman chroniclers, who frequently interrupt their works to ponder the lives of powerful, past and present monarchs. Three of these writers—Oderic Vitalis, Henry of Huntingdon, and William of Malmesbury—each pause to study the overwhelming impact of rulers like William the Conqueror and the ephemeral nature of their moments of power.[3] Fascinated by the interplay of individual wills and the external forces of fortune and providence, these writers draw attention to the precariousness of human experience.

With the renewal of interest in classical myth and ancient story in the late Middle Ages and early Renaissance, many writers systematically began to catalog the stories of famous heroes scattered in various texts and traditions. Among these, Petrarch and Boccaccio are particularly important, Petrarch for his distinction between biblical and classical matter and his historical sense of the classical past, Boccaccio for the systematic and comprehensive nature of his compilations. In three encyclopediac works—*De casibus illustrium virorum, De claris mulieribus,* and *De genealogia deorum*[4]—Boccaccio gathers together, and thereby preserves from oblivion, the bulk of ancient stories of illustrious men and women. The *De casibus* (1358), which is the ultimate source of Lydgate's poem, is an account of the fall from fortune of the great men in the Bible, myth, legend, and history, either as a result of their own sins or as a result of the activities of the capricious goddess Fortuna. The purpose of retelling the stories is to teach princes the lessons of wisdom and virtue by exempla and to warn them of the mutability of earthly experience. Boccaccio's account was extremely popular in the fourteenth and fifteenth centuries and survives in eighty-five manuscripts. At the request of the duke of Berry, Laurent de Premierfait, a writer attached to the court of Charles V, undertook a translation of the *De Casibus,* completing a first version of the poem in 1400 and a much longer second version in 1409. In this version, which is Lydgate's, Laurent pads the narrative with factual, moral, and mythological digressions so that his text swells to almost double the size of Boccaccio's. Laurent's amplification was appreciated by his contemporaries, including Lydgate, who praises him in his prologue to the *Fall of Princes* for his rhetoric and for his patience in clarifying the meaning of his narrative by his digressions (prologue ll. 36 ff.).

Poet and Patron

In 1431, Lydgate's long-term patron, Humphrey, duke of Gloucester, commissioned him to translate Laurent's poem. Humphrey, a prominent figure in the political arena of the second quarter of the fifteenth century, was the younger brother of Henry V and the protector of England during the minority of Henry VI. Married to Jacqueline of Hainault in 1422, he became the political rival of the powerful Henry Beaufort and William de la Pole, earl of Suffolk, who finally in 1447 had Humphrey arrested and imprisoned. Lydgate's close association with Humphrey dates from at least 1422, when he wrote the poem on Gloucester's impending marriage.[5] Before this time, Lydgate and Gloucester shared a common circle of acquaintances through the household of Thomas Chaucer and through the Abbey of Bury St. Edmund itself. In his prologue, Lydgate refers to Humphrey's political position and praises him for his integrity and continued struggle against the Lollards:

> Thus is he bothe manli and eek wis,
> Chose off God to been his owyn knyht,
> And off o thyng he hath a synguler pris,
> That heretik dar noon come in his siht,
> In Cristis feith he stant so hool vpriht,
> Off hooli chirche diffence and champioun,
> To chastise alle that do therto tresoun.
>
> (prologue, ll. 407–13)

In addition to his activities as a politician and statesman, Humphrey also played an active role in the introduction of humanism into England. In his prologue, Lydgate paints a picture of his patron as a serious scholar who kept company with learned men and clerks:

> [He] hath gret ioye with clerkis to comune:
> And no man is mor expert off language,
> Stable in study alwey he doth contune,
> . . . .
> And natwithstandyng his staat & dignite,
> His corage neuer doth appalle
> To studie in bookis off antiquite,
> Therin he hath so gret felicite
> Vertuously hymsilff to ocupie,
> Off vicious slouthe to haue the maistrie.
> (prologue, ll. 387–99)

Humphrey, in fact, did much to bring Italian scholars and texts to England. Although his motives were often political and self-serving, he nevertheless was one of the most important patrons of Italian scholars in England and English writers in the first half of the fifteenth century.

Hammond reveals that Humphrey's involvement in Lydgate's translation of the *Fall of Princes* went beyond the ordinary role of patron and benefactor.[6] Humphrey appears to have made an effort to oversee the translation at several points, and, in the epilogues to books 2 and 3, Lydgate describes his fear of the duke's displeasure. Humphrey also repeatedly lent Lydgate texts to be worked into his version of the *Fall,* for example, the *Policraticus* of John of Salisbury, a text that Humphrey had in his own library and which Lydgate interpolates into book II (ll. 827 ff.). Similarly, in book 2, Lydgate adds a translation of the *Declamatio* of Lucretia by Coluccio Salutati, a famous Italian humanist and acquaintance of Petrarch, at the request of his patron. Although he had earlier refused to tell the story of Lucretia in detail (2.978) out of deference to his master Chaucer, at Humphrey's urging he later narrates the tale at length.[7] Finally, Lydgate indicates, Humphrey requested that he add envoys to each chapter of Laurent's poem (2.145), a significant change in his version.

As Lydgate's prologues and epilogues imply, Humphrey may have been more generous with his suggestions than with his financial support. Although his praise of his patron is enthusiastic in the opening prologue, it becomes more tempered by the third book, where Lydgate amplifies Boccaccio to emphasize his poverty and plead for aid (3.64–70). Hammond speculates that between the first and third books, Lydgate also wrote Humphrey a short begging poem, the "Letter to Gloucester," in the tradition of Chaucer's "Complaint to his Purse."[8] Again, at the end of book 3 of the *Fall of Princes,* Lydgate adds a "Chapitle on the governance of Poetis" in which he emphasizes poets' dependence on the generosity of their patrons and concludes with a request for money. We have no evidence of any more help from Humphrey, and Lydgate's friend Shirley testifies to the poet's burdensome poverty in MS Add. 16165 and MS Add. 29729.[9] The *Fall* ends with a final tired plea for aid, this time to the Lord God to send his book "miht, grace and prosperite" (l. 3603).

Boccaccio, Laurent, and Lydgate

In the *Fall of Princes,* Lydgate undertakes a bolder and more ambitious scheme than he had in the *Troy Book* and the *Siege of Thebes.* In dealing with Laurent's text, he not only amplifies, but revises considerably, changing the point of view and emphasis of his sources. Boccaccio's version is essentially a history of Fortune, an account of the blows the goddess has dealt to noble characters from the time of Adam and Eve to the fourteenth century. The structure of the work is that of a processional of figures, viewed in alternation as single portraits from close up and as a group of characters from a distance. By accumulating repeated examples of man's fall from prosperity, Boccaccio emphasizes the mutability of Fortune in the world, and, in numerous digressions, he warns man to avoid putting too much trust in earthly things. As he suggests in his preface, he writes to provide examples of the behavior of noble men and women at the high and low points of their Fortune to serve as lessons for the profit of his readers.[10] Laurent likewise turns his attention to the activities of Fortune. In translating, he claims that his purpose is to improve, "muer la chose en mieulx," by clarifying the meaning of Boccaccio's words.[11] To some extent, Laurent's additions destroy the pattern and rhythm of Boccaccio's version with their repeated glossing, commentary, and moralizing.

Lydgate moves further away from Boccaccio's original design in his version by directing the *Fall of Princes* more explicitly as a manual of advice for rulers. While the *De casibus* and the *Des cas des nobles hommes et femmes* focus on Fortune, the main emphasis of the *Fall of Princes* is on the conduct of the ruler and his ability to profit from the examples he witnesses. To this end, Lydgate transforms many of the individual stories into practical examples of princely qualities to emulate and vices to eschew. Neither openly contemptuous of the rulers of his age like Boccaccio, nor deferential and obsequious like Laurent, Lydgate manipulates his material to avoid passages that might undermine the position of a monarch, but at the same time, he firmly reminds the ruler of his powers, his limitations, and his supreme obligation to govern well.

A good example of Lydgate's change in emphasis is provided by the story of Atreus and Thyestes in book 1.[12] In Boccaccio's and Laurent's versions, this story is one of sheer horror, a chilling example of Fortune's cruelty. As Boccaccio is about to relate the tale of Duke Theseus, Thyestes suddenly appears before him and orders him to tell his tragedy first, for there was never one more terrible. He then recounts his change of fortune, his dispute with his brother, and Atreus' gruesome revenge. Once a powerful king, Thyestes ended powerless and betrayed, drinking the blood of his three slain children. In describing this scene, Laurent adds even more gory details than Boccaccio, relating at length how Atreus himself murdered the three innocent children and took their blood from their throats, how he presented their bodies to Thyestes at a grand banquet, "les aucuns cuytz en eaue, les autres rostis sur les charbons,"[13] gave Thyestes their blood to drink to quench his thirst, and for dessert presented their heads.[14] Again, in relating Atreus' version of the story, Laurent provides a graphic account of the crime, narrating at length his and Thyestes' horrible deeds.[15]

Lydgate, in contrast, tones down the spectacular nature of the scene, omitting most of the disgusting and distracting details of Atreus' crime and instead focuses squarely on the practical lesson to be learned from the event. Before he presents the actual banquet, in a dramatic passage which he weaves into the story, he warns against being tricked by fraud hidden under an honest face:

> There is no damage in comparisoun,
> That may be likned, bi no rassemblaunce,
> To feyned trouthe and symulacioun,
> Whan fraude is hid with a fair contenaunce,
> Pretendyng trouthe outward bi disseyuaunce,

And vndirnethe, off most fals entent,
Off doubilnesse darith the serpent.
(1.3956–62)[16]

Having provided a moral context, he then presents the banquet scene, which we now see clearly as an example of the dangers of fraud. Finally, in the envoy (1.4215–42), he warns princes specifically about brotherly strife "Hatful to God and contrary onto kynde" and concludes with a passionate outburst against deceit.

Likewise, Lydgate revises many of the digressions in his sources to make his version more effective as a manual for princes. A striking example is provided by his treatment of Laurent's "Chapter on Good Government."[17] While Laurent develops this section primarily to censure the behavior of proud princes and to warn that they too are subject to Fortune, Lydgate introduces a much broader vision of the proper relation among the various parts of the state. To emphasize the crucial reliance of the prince upon his subjects, he adapts and expands the famous body-state image from John of Salisbury's *Policraticus*.[18]

Second, Lydgate reshapes the *Fall of Princes* to link sin more closely with man's downfall. In the prologue to book 1, for example, he considerably expands his source to articulate this theme at length. While the Latin text is only fifteen lines and Laurent's translation forty-seven very short lines, Lydgate's version extends for more than 160 lines. In contrast to both Boccaccio and Laurent, who use the prologue to emphasize the difference between good men who must be reminded only once of the evil deeds of the vicious and others who need to be warned by repeated example, Lydgate reworks this passage to define the crucial relation between virtue and prosperity. Adding to his source, he suggests that the stories he translates serve as "lanterns" to others to warn them of the vices they should eschew. He then introduces the critical point that is absent in Boccaccio's and Laurent's versions: men are rewarded according to their desserts. Those who follow virtue will endure the longest:

The fall off on is a cleer lanterne
To teche a-nother what he shal eschewe;
Pereil off on, is, who can discerne,
Scoole and doctryn from pereil to remewe.
As men disserue such guerdoun ther mut sewe;

> In vice nor vertu no man may God deceyue,
> Lik ther desertis ther meede thei [shal] receyue.
>
> Who folweth vertu lengest doth perseuere,
> Be it in richesse, be it in pouerte. . . .
> (2.29–37)

It is not Fortune who causes princes to fall but sinful behavior, for Fortune has little power over princes who are governed by virtue (2.43–56). Lydgate reinforces the emphasis of this prologue by his revisions of several of the stories, for example, in the tales of the Sardanapalus, Balthasar, Xerxes, Machaeus, and Olympias among others.[19]

But his change in point of view is seen most dramatically in a conspicuous category of additions which he weaves into his source—the story of the churl rising to power. Lydgate introduces this kind of example a number of times when a different emphasis is warranted by his sources, most notably in the stories of Marcius Manlius, Agathocles, Sandrodoctus, Andriscus, and Spartacus.[20] In each case, he exploits the story to point up the relation between innate viciousness and a character's downfall. While, for example, Boccaccio and Laurent narrate the experience of the tyrant Agathocles to show that Fortune not only uses her power against high estates, but often raises low-born to a position of power only to destroy them, Lydgate develops the tale as an example of the vulnerability of the vicious when raised to power. Prefacing his account with an interpolation of sixty-nine lines, he explains:

> On the most contrarious myscheeff
> Founde in this erthe, bi notable euidence,
> Is onli this: bi fortunat violence
> Whan that a wrech[e], cherlissh of nature,
> Thestat of princis vnwarli doth recure.
> (4.2656–60)

No one has more presumption than a vicious churl raised to a high position. Lydgate thus bids us beware of "fals coinage," viciousness hidden under a fair and powerful cover. Finally, he relates the story of Agathocles by way of example and concludes by emphasizing the increased severity of his fall because of his churlishness.

Fortune and the Fall of Princes

Although Lydgate's prologue to book 2 and his treatment of many of the stories indicate that sin rather than Fortune is the cause of man's downfall, he does not suggest that man can overcome Fortune with certainty by being virtuous. Fortune in the *Fall of Princes* is still capricious. She visits her calamities on all men, at times justly, at times without apparent reason. But Lydgate emphasizes, in contrast to his sources, that a prince is much more vulnerable to Fortune if he is sinful.[21] He explains:

> Hasti risyng, & thrifft that is sodeyne,
> And surmountyng bi violent rauyne,
> And extort poweer, may for a tyme atteyne
> In riche chaier of lordshipe for to shyne.
> Sodeyn ascendyng doth sodenli declyne;
> And bi vntrouthe, wher-euer ther be encres,
> Men waite of custum a sodeyn disencres.
> (4.2906–12)

Fortune in the *Fall of Princes* finally appears both as a source of retribution for man's pride, disobedience, lasciviousness, and duplicity, and as an unpredictable and even arbitrary doler of punishment. In stanzas which he adds to the story of Hercules, for example, Lydgate indicates that Hercules precipitated his own change in Fortune by the "soote venym, the sauouri fals poisoun" of his licentiousness (1.5524). Fortune's blows represent the fate Hercules deserved for his devotion to false love (1.5531–37). But in dealing with the story of Oedipus, Lydgate amplifies Laurent's and Boccaccio's accounts to link Oedipus' fate with the whims of Fortune, "ay double in her werkyng" (1.3277–83). Again, in concluding the story of Theseus, Lydgate emphasizes the uncertainty of man's prosperity, for when it suits Fortune, she will turn their "sugre" into "bittir gall" (1.4550). The only constant that emerges in Lydgate's treatment is that Fortune affects all men, princes and subjects, high-born and low-born. Her activity reveals that all earthly things are transitory. Princes' power, worldly prosperity, human happiness are ephemeral under Fortune's sway. Lydgate thus directs man's attention to the stability of God, urging him to profit by the examples of great men and turn away from "Worldli glorie veyn and ful onstable."

The Rise and Fall of Civilization

Even more significant than Lydgate's changes in emphasis in the *Fall of Princes* is his effort to expand, both thematically and formally, the scope of the individual stories to create a larger backdrop for the various exempla than we find in his sources. In amplifying Boccaccio's and Laurent's narratives, he enlarges their focus to move beyond the moral and political contexts of the kings' mirror. Particularly in the later books, he develops a successively expanding structure, large and open ended in its form, which provides the vehicle for an examination of the design of human history.

In part, Lydgate reshapes his narrative by means of the envoys which he adds to the stories. Set off from the rest of the poem by their style, meter, rhyme scheme, and refrains, these passages serve to direct the reader's attention beyond the individual tales to the larger patterns that underlie the action of the poem. They define a vision of history as a rising and falling of civilizations with each individual life as a fleeting image in the tabloid. Typical of Lydgate's treatment is the envoy to the story of Gideon in book 1 (3102–29). This envoy is a brief four stanzas, but Lydgate efficiently exploits each section to develop his theme. In the first stanza, he moves from the story to the general theme of the envoy—the transitoriness of the world: "Mihti Princis, remembre that your power / Is transitory & no while a-bidyng" (1.3102). In the next two stanzas, Lydgate enlarges this theme by means of two striking images—the setting sun and the changing seasons (1.3109–22). Finally, in an increasingly solemn tone, he emphasizes the universality of worldly change: "Al ertheli blisse dependith in a weer, / In a ballaunce oneuenli hangyng. . . ." His refrain word "declyne," given greater prominence by his exploitation of the same three rhymes in each stanza, provides a dramatic echo of his theme and defines the movement of each of the preceding stanzas. The note sounded by this passage recurs in the majority of the envoys and provides a recurrent reminder of the transitoriness of the world and of the need for great moral strength, even if man is virtuous, in order to combat Fortune. The envoys thus create lyric moments that punctuate the action of the poem and draw attention to the design against which we must view the individual stories.

Lydgate makes a further effort to direct the reader's attention beyond the scope of the individual stories by his manipulation of the major structural units of the narrative. In delineating the separate books of the poem, he places the stories in the largest earthly context possible, the downfall of all civilization. The design is first articulated in the magnificent envoy to Rome which closes book 2. In this passage, which stands off from the rest of the narrative and from many of the other envoys as well by its tone and style, Lydgate reminds the Romans of their foundation in dissension, slaughter, and robbery and warns them of their imminent ruin if they do not change their ways. In the next seven stanzas, he briefly reviews Roman history in the form of a moving *ubi sunt* catalog of all its dead heroes:

> Wher be thyn Emperours, most souereyn off renoun?
> Kynges exiled for outraious lyuyng?
> Thi senatours, with worthi Scipioun?
> Poetis olde thi tryumphes rehersyng,
> Thi laureat knyhtis, most statli ther ridyng,
> Thyn aureat glorie, thy noblesse tenlumyne,
> Is be long processe brouht onto ruyne.
>
> (2.4467–73)

The glory of Rome is ephemeral; neither its conquerors nor its poets will prevent it from being "brouht onto ruyne."

Books 6–8 gradually enlarge this pattern by moving from the separate stories to the possible destruction of all civilization. Book 6 depicts the downfall of order represented by imperial Rome. The action begins with the story of Saturnine who caused great trouble in Rome by conspiring with Marius to banish Metellus. Then follows a number of stories of people who attacked Rome, including Marius, Spartacus, Viriathus, and Mithridates, and finally an account of the bitter feud of Pompey and Caesar that threatened the downfall of the city. The series ends with the brief but impressive reaffirmation of order through the eloquence of Cicero and the beginning of a new cycle under the Triumvirs.

The panorama widens in book 7 as Lydgate presents, in a long passage which he adds to his source, the further degeneration of Rome against the backdrop of the former Golden Age. In contrast to the present state:

Ther was that tyme no wrong nor violence,
Envie exiled from eueri creature,
Dissolucioun & dronken insolence,
Ribaudie & al swich foul ordure,
Froward surfetis, contrarye to nature,
Ibanished wern, because attemperaunce
Hadde in that world hooli the gouernaunce.

Youthe was bridled vndir disciplyne,
Vertuous studie floured in myddil age,
Dreed heeld the yerde of norture & doctrine,
Riot restreyned from surquedous outrage,
Hatful detracccioun repressid his langage,
Kouth was charite, because attemperaunce
Hadde in that world hooli gouernaunce.
(7.1160–73)

This order did not last "because attemp[e]raunce / Was set aside and lost her gouernaunce." Lydgate then moves from the age of gold through the ages of silver, lead, iron, and copper to the present and concludes with two noble examples—John the Baptist and Diogenes—who each in his own way preserves the values of the age of gold and contrasts sharply with the present rulers of Rome. Book 7 ends with the downfall of Jerusalem and a still wider panorama of human destruction.

Near the end of book 8, Lydgate again expands his vision to include all known civilizations. Adding to his source he warns that not only Rome and Jerusalem, but Babylon, Persia, Troy, Carthage, and all of the ancient world fell as a result of the misconduct of the rulers and the recklessness of the people.[22] Bringing his survey up to the present day, he concludes with the more recent example of the divisions in France.[23] Finally, by implication at the end of the chapter he extends this design to England, reminding his countrymen of the example of Arthur brought low by the strife between him and Mordred, and concludes with a relevant warning against division in a realm.[24]

Like the earlier Golden Age, the flourishing of Arthurian chivalry in Lydgate's version represents a high point of civilization, a moment of harmony and order in the realm. Argus, Hector, and Ulysses in one (8.2797–99), Arthur, the model knight, inspired honor, justice, and liberality among his subjects. His knights defended the innocent, protected the weak, and fought to preserve their country and the church. The true light of chivalry shone in his reign. But, like the original Golden Age and like the civilizations of Troy, Rome, Carthage, Jerusalem, and Alexandria, this order too was destroyed by the caprice of Fortune and by the treachery of men. Lydgate concludes with a vision of the desolation of Britain and the light of the Round Table eclipsed (8.3886 ff.).

In book 9, Lydgate represents the modern period as a fall from the high point of the Golden Age and the ideals of Arthurian civilization. Amassing numerous examples, he reveals the disorder and misrule of modern rulers in both church and state. The examples in this book are bleaker than those in the earlier books. Few of the characters attain the magnificent tragic stature of the old heroes—Oedipus, Hercules, Caesar, Alexander, or Arthur. Rather, Lydgate emphasizes their pettiness, malice, and perversity—the cruelty of Brunhilde, the viciousness of Pope John II, the inconstancy of Frederick II, the presumption of Philippa Catanensi, among other examples. We are left with a vision of the degeneration of human greatness.

Poetry and Fortune

The activity of the poet is placed in opposition to the workings of Fortune and the rise and fall of civilizations. In the *Fall of Princes,* Lydgate reiterates his earlier view of the poet as an ennobler of men. An "enluminer" who sheds light on his matter by means of his rhetoric and eloquence, the poet reproves vice and encourages men to choose virtue by his examples:

> Ther cheeff labour is vicis to repreve
> With a maner couert symylitude,
> And non estat with ther langage greeve
> Bi no rebukyng of termys dul and rude;
> What-euer thei write, on vertu ay conclude,
> Appeire no man in no maner wise:
> This thoffise of poetis that be wise.
>
> (3.3830–36)

But Lydgate goes beyond this definition in the later books of the *Fall of Princes.* Adding to Boccaccio in the prologue to book 4,

Lydgate hints that poetry has the power to withstand the ravages of Fortune and remain fresh and enduring:

> Fruit of writyng set in cronicles olde,
> Most delectable of fresshnesse in tastyng,
> And most goodli & glorious to beholde,
> In cold and heete lengest abidyng,
> Chaung of cesouns may doon it non hyndryng,
> And wher-so be that men dyne or faste,
> The mor men taste, the lenger it wil laste.
> (4.1–7)

While Fortune brings discord, strife, and disorder, poetry leads men to a civilized and harmonious state.[25]

In book 6, Lydgate develops in some detail a view of poetry as the antidote to the destructive effects of Fortune. Following his sources, he begins with a debate between Boccaccio and Fortuna that defines the terms of the conflict. Fortuna argues that it is her nature to be changeable and that Boccaccio must accept her as she is and not complain of her doubleness. Boccaccio responds by comparing the destructive effects of Fortuna with the beneficial effects of poetry. While Fortuna creates strife and discord, "fair langage" and the "fressh ditees" of poetry bring men into harmony and prevent their kingdoms and cities from being destroyed (6.375–78). To clinch his arguments, Lydgate adds to Laurent's and Boccaccio's narratives a reference to Amphion. Warning Fortuna that the power of poetry and eloquent language is considerable, the narrator cites the example of Amphion, who by means of his "fair langage" first civilized men:

> Philisophres of the goldene ages
> And poetes that fond out fressh ditees,
> As kyng Amphioun with his fair langages
> And with his harpyng made folk of louh degrees,
> As laborers, tenhabite first cites;—
> And so bi musik and philosophie
> Gan first of comouns noble policie.
> (6.337–43)

Reorganizing Boccaccio's structure, Lydgate adds a further reference to Amphion at the end of book 6 to emphasize the power of the rhetorician to join warring parties and bring comfort and harmony:

> Bexaumple as Amphioun, with song & elloquence
> Bilte the wallis of Thebes the cite,
> He hadde of rhetorik so gret subtilite.
>
> In his language ther was so gret plesaunce,
> Fyndyng therbi so inli gret proffit,
> That al the contre kam to his obeissaunce. . . .
> (6.3491–96)

The pattern of the stories within the body of book 6 reiterates the opposition of Fortuna and "fair langage." The stories describe the downfall of civilization, represented by imperial Rome, through chaos and disorder and the reaffirmation of the power of rhetoric and poetry in the career of Cicero. Lydgate first introduces a series of examples of people who, with Fortuna's help, created internal disorder or war against the city, including Saturninus, Drusus, Fanticus, Spartacus, Viriathus, Marius, Mithriadates, Adrian, Pompey, and Brutus. Juxtaposed to these stories is the example of Cicero, who restored peace to Rome by his eloquence and saved the city from ruin: "Thoruh his langage this saide Tullius / Reconsilede bi his soote orisouns, / To the lordshipe & grace of Iulius, / Princes, kynges of dyuers regiouns, / That suspect stood bi accusaciouns" (6.3130–34). For a short time, the power of eloquent language triumphs, but Cicero is ultimately exiled and killed. The book ends with the beginning of a new order under the Triumvirs.

In his prologue, Boccaccio extends the conflict to his own writing. Although Fortuna has warned him that his effort is futile and that all is under her sway, Boccaccio determines to continue his work and by his writing inspire men to a state of virtue removed from Fortune's domain. Modifying his text, Lydgate goes even further than Boccaccio as he emphasizes not only the poet's power but his responsibility to write:

> . . . he that can and ceseth for to write
> Notable exaumples of our predecessours,
> Of envie men wil hym atwite,
> That he in gardyns leet pershe þe holsum flours
> In sondry caas that myhte do gret soccours.
> (8.162–66)

In Lydgate's view, it is the poet's profound duty to persist despite all obstacles in his task as an orderer of man.

The Influence of the *Fall of Princes*

The vision of the poet's activity as ennobling, a source of order and harmony in the state, and the expansive structure Lydgate develops in the *Fall of Princes* had a continued influence in the Renaissance. The poem was popular both as an exemplary history and as a sourcebook of memorable passages. More than thirty manuscripts of the complete poem survive, including some lavishly decorated and expensive copies.[26] The *Fall* had a large circulation in the sixteenth century in the printed editions of Pynson (1495, 1527), Tottel (1554), and Wayland (1558). Edwards points out that several editors also selected portions of the poem, for example, the envoys and the passages on women, for anthology collections.[27] These manuscripts, extremely popular in the fifteenth and sixteenth centuries, include the Shirley MSS Ashmole 59 and Trinity R.3.20 and other important manuscripts like Trinity R.3.19. Stanzas of the *Fall* were also incorporated into copies of Chaucer's *Monk's Tale,* for example, in Trinity R.3.19 and in Renaissance didactic works like Peter Idley's *Instruction to his Son.*

Lydgate's Renaissance audience valued the *Fall of Princes* as a mirror from which they could extrapolate lessons about the fate of great men and draw examples of the patterns in history. Several attempts were made to give the poem a new relevance in the large-scale continuations of the *Fall* which appeared throughout the sixteenth century. The most important of these works, the *Mirror for Magistrates,* develops both the material of Lydgate's narrative, extending his coverage up to the Elizabethan era, and its amplificatory style.[28] Like Lydgate's *Fall,* the Renaissance versions are expansive and open-ended in their structures and provide an obvious departure from the enclosed forms characteristic of the Ricardian poets, for example, the hierarchical structure of Gower's *Confessio Amantis,* the series of framed stories in Chaucer's *Canterbury Tales,* and the increasingly inward and circular journey of Langland's *Piers Plowman.* Unlike these poets, Lydgate creates an expansive structure punctuated by conspicuous high moments, which develops its material by a repeated enlarging of its scale and scope. His work popularizes a form and matter that remains important in the two centuries after his up through the history plays of Shakespeare.[29]

Chapter Five

Laureate Lydgate: Public and Political Poems

In the years between the composition of the Troy and Thebes narratives and the *Fall of Princes,* Lydgate moves into an increasingly public and political arena. No longer primarily a poet of the courtly mode, he takes on the role of an unofficial laureate, a poet who is available to commemorate important occasions and events and serve the needs of prominent patrons. His output during this period is extremely varied, ranging from poems for weddings and other celebrations, to New Year and holiday poems, to elevated coronation pieces, to official propaganda and word pictures of important events. In his public and occasional poems, Lydgate reveals himself to be an extremely versatile poet who often skillfully accommodates his poetic concerns to the demands of the occasion. Although at times he simply appears to be writing to order, in the most successful of his public poems, Lydgate creates a work or artifact that endures beyond the immediate bounds of the occasion.

Noble and Bourgeois Patrons

One of the most important of the early patrons of Lydgate's occasional poetry was Thomas Chaucer, the son of the poet, Geoffrey Chaucer. Thomas, an important statesman and prominent figure in his own right, was M.P. for Oxfordshire and Speaker of the House of Commons on several occasions between 1400 and 1430 and between 1424 and 1425 member of the Council. Like his father, Thomas was employed on frequent diplomatic missions abroad. In June 1414, for example, he was commissioned to treat with the ambassadors of the duke of Burgundy in an attempt to arrange the marriage of Henry V and Catherine of Valois.[1] Again in October 1417, he was sent to negotiate with the ambassadors of the French king for a final settlement of the war. After serving in the field for Henry in France between 1417 and 1419, Thomas Chaucer returned to France in July 1420 to treat with the lieutenant of Brittany about the observance of the king's final peace.[2] Finally, he was chief butler to Henry IV, V, and VI.

It is unclear which of Chaucer's diplomatic missions prompted Lydgate's poem. Each has been suggested at one time or another by critics.[3] In its form, "On the Departing of Thomas Chaucer" is indebted to the classical *propemticon* or poem which anticipates a prosperous voyage.[4] But the opening prayer to Lucyna and Neptune to protect Thomas Chaucer from adversity also echoes Aurelius' appeal in the *Franklin's Tale*[5] and the poem introduces several other Chaucerian allusions. Thomas is given many of the virtues of Chaucer's admirable characters, the "fredom" and courtesy of the Knight, the jovial nature and reputation for hospitality of the Franklin, and Lydgate sums up his picture by echoing the Franklin's portrait:

> Saint Iulyan, oure ioye and al our glorye,
> Come hoom ageyne, lyche as we desyre.
> To suppowaylen al þe hole shyre.
> (ll. 68–70)

Technically, Lydgate handles the material he borrows with considerable skill. The poem progresses from the opening invocation for Chaucer's safe voyage to the effect on those left behind as the "agreable sonne / Of housholding and fulsum haboundaunce / Eclipsid is" (ll. 22–24), to the poet's consolation and prayer for Chaucer's speedy return. Each stanza is carefully crafted. By means of alliteration, internal echoing, word pairings, and coinages, Lydgate creates a stately and dignified effect. The first stanza, with its conspicuous reduplication and echoing of sounds, is typical of his treatment:

> O þow Lucyna, qwene of empyresse
> Of waters alle and of floodes rage,
> And cleped art lady and goddesse
> Of iorneying and fortunate passage,
> Governe and guye by grace þe viage,
> þow heuenly qween, sith I of hert[e] prey,
> My maystre Chaucer goodly to convey.
> (ll. 1–7)

In Shirley's copy, the love lyric "My Lady Dere" is attached to the "Ballade" as Thomas's parting gift to his wife, but one cannot establish this connection with certainty.

Lydgate's association with the household of Thomas Chaucer also brought him into contact with three other influential patrons for his occasional poems—Humphrey, duke of Gloucester, and the earls of Warwick and Salisbury. Humphrey, in addition to his role in the composition of the *Fall of Princes,* commissioned Lydgate to write a poem in celebration of his impending marriage to Countess Jacqueline of Hainault and Holland (1422).[6] A politically delicate subject, Gloucester's marriage and his subsequent claim to Hainault strained the Anglo-Burgundian alliance which was the basis of the foreign policy of his rival, Henry Beaufort, and threatened the hope for lasting peace with France. Lydgate shrewdly downplays the political aspects of the marriage and solves the difficult problem of his subject matter by celebrating love and marriage as a prelude to peace. The first half of the poem presents marriage as the "grounde and cause" of peace and unity in countries (ll. 39–40). Inspired by Venus, Cupid, and Jupiter, regions, provinces, and nations joined with each other in "þe knotte of allyaunce" (l. 15). Lydgate concludes this section of the poem with examples of marriages instrumental in obtaining peace, including the union of Henry V and Queen Katherine, daughter of Charles VI of France. He prays that the marriage of Gloucester and Jacqueline of Hainault will be another such union and put an end to "al rancour" in both lands (l. 62). In the second half of the poem, Lydgate treats Jacqueline and Humphrey as exemplary figures, the contemporary counterparts of his catalog of heroic women and men. The poem ends with a prayer that good fortune prevail in the land as a result of the marriage of two such noble figures. Lydgate's hopes for Gloucester and Jacqueline of Hainault did not come to fruition, however, for Gloucester soon lost interest in Jacqueline. By 1428, he had obtained a divorce from his wife in order to marry Eleanor Cobham, one of her ladies-in-waiting. This behavior provoked considerable protest, including a poem tenuously attributed to Lydgate, the "Complaint for my Lady of Gloucester" (1428).[7]

A less controversial patron associated with the household of Thomas Chaucer was Thomas Montacute, the earl of Salisbury and second husband of Alice, Thomas Chaucer's daughter. Salisbury, perhaps at Alice's suggestion, commissioned Lydgate's translation of the

Pilgrimage of the Life of Man in 1426 when the two men were in Paris. The ornate dedication copy of the poem suggests that Lydgate must have regarded the assignment as a considerable honor, for Montacute not only was a prominent political figure but a poet of some reputation in his own right.[8] Equally important was Lydgate's relation with Richard de Beauchamp, count of Warwick (1382–1439). Even more than Gloucester and Salisbury, Warwick attempted to involve Lydgate's pen in political and propagandist activity. While Lydgate was still in Paris, Warwick, who was then serving as "lieutenant for the field in the absence of the regent Bedford," commissioned him to write "The Title and Pedigree of Henry VI."[9] This poem, which Lydgate tells us in his prologue is a translation of the pedigrees of Henry VI composed by a French scholar, Laurence Calot, at the command of the duke of Bedford, was written on 28 July 1427 to teach people the truth about the descent of the French crown (ll. 1–10).

The body of the poem begins with the argument that the dauphin, by his treacherous murder of Duke John of Burgundy, forfeited his rights to the throne. In his place, God sent Henry V, a worthy ruler and descendant of St. Louis, to govern France. By the force of the Treaty of Troyes and by his marriage to Katherine of France, he is the legitimate heir to the throne. After the deaths of the kings of England and France in close succession, Henry V has a double claim to the French crown through his mother's and his father's lines. With an elaborate astrological flourish, Lydgate amends his version of Calot's genealogy, praising Henry and beseeching God to give him a long life. In all, Lydgate's energy in this poem seems oddly misplaced. His praise of Calot is compendious and his explanations of the reasons for his endeavor and the planetary influences are repetitive and uninspired. The poem apparently was accompanied by a magnificently drawn genealogical tree which served as a pictorial supplement to the text.

Warwick's daughter, Margaret, by his first wife, who later married John Talbot, earl of Shrewsbury, continued her family's support of Lydgate by commissioning him to write the history of *Guy of Warwick* (ca. 1425).[10] The poem, an ancestral romance in seventy-four ballad stanzas, narrates the story of the founder of the noble family, the chivalrous pilgrim Guy of Warwick, who in Athelstan's time (927 A.D.) saved the English from devastation by the Danes by fighting, in single combat, the champion Colebrand the Great.

Drawing upon the Latin chronicle of Gerardus Cornubiensis, Lydgate recounts Guy's return to England in answer to Athelstan's prayers, his entry into the country in disguise, the king's prophetic vision of Guy's activities as champion, the meeting of the king and Guy at an old hospital for the indigent, the contest itself, and the revelation of Guy's identity, his return to his family, and his eventual death. Although the work is not of exceptional poetic merit, it nevertheless is a competent and strategically planned version, designed to honor the Warwick family. Lydgate follows his source closely, focusing on the historical part of the story and omitting some of the romance features and material of local interest. At several points, he amplifies considerably, giving the story a distinct didactic emphasis. For example, he adds a long digression (sts. 5–11) which links the troubles in England with God's punishment for the sins of the people and the arrival of Guy as a result of His mercy. Similarly, he introduces the prayer of Athelstan (st. 27) which emphasizes the English need for help, links Guy's return explicitly with God's intervention, and stylistically elevates and emotionalizes the action. Finally, he expands the adventures of Guy (sts. 33–72) by means of scriptural and mythological allusions to heighten the valor and nobility of his hero.

In Lydgate's version, the king and hero thus gain greater prominence as protectors of the realm. Their position reinforces the views of the "Pedigree" and the *Siege of Thebes* about the relation of the ruler to his people and the dangers of external claims to the crown. Lydgate's emphasis would have been particularly flattering to Richard de Beauchamp, who drew attention to his descent from the legendary Guy of Warwick.[11] Lydgate composed a final poem for the Warwick family for Beauchamp's third wife Isabella, "Fifteen Joys of Our Lady," more appropriately considered with the devotional poetry in the next chapter.

Royal Patrons

But Lydgate's most illustrious patroness was Henry's widow, the queen-mother Katherine for whom he wrote two pieces, a "Valentine to her that Excelleth All" and "That now is Hay some-tyme was grase."[12] The "Valentine," probably written before 1425 and the queen's association with Owen Tudor, contains twenty Chaucerian stanzas that build up to the poet's choice of the one true Valentine, the Virgin. Listing the noble qualities of famous women in the Bible, in poetry, and in history, he suggests, by his refrain, "But I love oon whiche excelliþe alle," that he loves one who is more worthy. After praising the Virgin and her life, he turns to Queen Katherine, praying that Mary protect her and her son, Henry VI. With some originality, Lydgate thus combines an essentially traditional religious poem with a panegyric to the queen and infant king. The second poem to Katherine, Shirley tells us in his rubric, was "made at þe commaundment of þe Quene Kateryn as in here sportes she walkyd by the medowes that were late mowen in the monthe of Iulij." The poem, in the tradition of the *ubi sunt* lyrics, catalogs all of the earthly things that have faded—the spring flowers, the beauty of youth, the heroines of old, the Nine Worthies—and concludes that the world is changeable and transitory:

> Nowe thes tres blosome and blome,
> Nowe the leves fade and falle;
> Nowe suger, nowe swete synamone,
> Nowe tryakle, nowe bytar galle;
> Nowe youthe, nowe age þat dothe apall;
> Nowe ioye, nowe myrthe, nowe alas;
> And thynke a-mongest thes chaungis all
> That nowe is heye: some tyme was gras.
> (ll. 105–112)

Thus the poet bids man not to trust this world but to seek the next.

In addition to the poems he composed for Katherine, Lydgate also served the royal family as an official laureate at the coronations of the eleven-year-old King Henry VI at Westminster Abbey in 1429 and at Paris in 1431. The English coronation is recorded in the chronicles as an occasion of considerable ceremony and flourish.[13] On the day before he was crowned, Henry and a procession of knights, clergy, and civic authorities made their way through the streets of London, which were covered with carpets. Wine and other refreshments were offered to the crowd, and along Henry's route allegorical scenes were set up on stages erected for the occasion. The coronation itself took place on Sunday, 6 November, with Cardinal Beaufort presiding as Henry was crowned with the great crown of St. Edward. As the author of the *Brut* reports, two of the bishops assembled helped the king place the crown, "for hyt was ovyr hevy for him, for he was of tendyr age."[14] A sumptuous banquet and elaborate entertainment followed the ceremony and Lydgate was called into service to commemorate the events.

For the coronation Lydgate's poem "The Title and Pedigree of Henry VI" was apparently circulated again along with a new three-stanza poem, the "Roundel for the Coronation."[15] As poet-propagandist, Lydgate is primarily concerned in these poems with supporting the union of the crowns of England and France in the kingship of Henry VI. While the "Title and Pedigree" is polemical in its stance, the appended "Roundel" is celebratory. It rejoices in the kingship of Henry VI as a new branch of the fleur-de-lys, a union of the blood of St. Edward and St. Louis, and urges the young king to be wise, circumspect, and stable like his father. Lydgate treats this theme more elaborately in the "Ballade to King Henry VI upon his Coronation." According to Stow, this ballade was presented to Henry on the day of his coronation at Westminster.[16] The "Ballade" traces Henry's descent from the English and French saints, St. Edward and St. Louis, and the two great national heroes, Arthur and Charlemagne, and thus establishes his claim to the two thrones. But the bulk of the poem focuses on the definition of the ideal king, drawing his qualities from biblical, classical, and contemporary models. Instructing the young King Henry to be true in faith, honorable as a knight, and just and merciful as a ruler, Lydgate cites the examples of the wise kings Solomon and David who governed by "witt" and "heghe prudence" (l. 53). Like the rest of the Nine Worthies and the Roman heroes of old, he must be hardy and forceful in battle, and like Constantius and Sigismund, he must defend the church. The virtues of a good king come together in the climactic example of the young ruler's father, Henry V, and Lydgate concludes the body of the poem by urging him to benefit from the models of his father and mother.

The themes woven together in the "Pedigree," the "Roundel," and the "Ballade"—the justification of Henry's joint succession to the thrones of England and France, the definition of good kingship, and the vision of Henry V as an exemplary ruler—are emphasized in a decorative manner in "The Soteltes at the Coronation Banquet of Henry VI" (1432).[17] These "subtleties" were an artistic table decoration or dessert served after each of the main courses at the dinner. Like the pageants staged along the route of Henry's processional, the "soteltes" represented allegorically the political significance of Henry's succession. Accompanying each decoration was a tablet or scroll that contained Lydgate's brief verse elucidation of the significance of the figures, a companion piece or word-painting of the scene.

In a later poem, "King Henry VI's Triumphal Entry into London,"[18] Lydgate exaggerates many of the tendencies of the "Soteltes," providing a much more elaborate verbal counterpart to the occasion than he had in the earlier coronation poems. The poem is both experimental in its effort to create a poetic artifact or monument of the occasion and tedious in its attenuation. Lydgate's task in the "Triumphal"—to aggrandize and elevate the event for posterity—was a delicate one. In the same year as the coronation at Westminster, England's position in France grew weaker. In May, Joan of Arc defeated the English at Orleans and Patay and then marched to Rheims to crown Charles VII king. To solidify the remaining supporters of the English cause, Bedford planned to have Henry crowned with considerable ceremony in Paris. Before he reached Paris, Joan of Arc was taken prisoner at Compiègne, handed over to the English, tried, and burned at the stake. When Henry marched into Paris about six months later, he was received with an impressive show of pageantry including a colorful processional, *tableaux vivants,* and political allegories. But as several of the chroniclers emphasize, this display was not matched by the support of the Parisians, who, on the whole, proved apathetic and indifferent.[19]

To mitigate this failure, Lydgate was assigned the responsibility of overseeing the official welcome given to the king on his return to London and was expected not only to write the official poem but to design the tableaux and allegorical scenes that commemorated the event. In his effort, Lydgate worked closely with the town clerk, John Carpenter, a friend and former collaborator in the pictorial representation of Lydgate's *Danse Macabre* on the walls of the cloister of Pardon Churchyard near St. Paul's. Carpenter has left a detailed letter describing the processional, which early critics believed to be the source of Lydgate's poem but which is now generally recognized to be a separate version of the same events.[20] Both accounts describe how the king was welcomed at Blackheath by the mayor, the alderman, and the citizens of London and then led into the city past an elaborate series of allegorical scenes. At London Bridge stood a giant, flanked by two antelopes bearing the arms of England and France, who announced in an inscription that he would protect the king from foreign enemies. The second scene, erected at the middle of the bridge, represented three empresses, Nature, Grace, and Fortune, who offered gifts of strength, knowledge and prudence, and prosperity. At Cornhill the king passed the third pageant, a Tabernacle of Wisdom adorned with the seven liberal arts and their classical representatives. From there, he proceeded to a child, seated upon a throne, with three governesses, Mercy, Trouth, and Clemence, who offered the scripture, "Honour off kynges, in euery mannys siht, / Of comyn custum lovith equyte and riht" (ll. 298–99). The fifth scene, in Cheapside, depicted an earthly paradise complete with conduits of wine for the guests, which Lydgate emphasizes were filled with wine of "attemperaunce," good governance, "goode ffoysoun," and consolation. The last two pageants, at the cross in Cheapside and at the entrance to St. Paul's churchyard where the clergy were assembled, established the king's claim to the kingdoms of England and France and his divine protection. Lydgate concludes with a celebration of the city of London for the glorious reception offered to the king. In these final stanzas, his style becomes more elevated as he increases the alliteration, repetition of words, and internal echoing:

> Be gladde, O London! be gladde and make grete ioye,
> Citee of Citees, off noblesse precellyng,
> In thy bygynnynge called Newe Troye;
> For worthynesse thanke God off alle thyng,
> Which hast this day resseyved so thy Kyng,
> With many a signe and many an obseruance
> To encrese thy name by newe remembraunce.
> (ll. 510–16)

The pageants, as Lydgate organizes them, thus both welcome the king and instruct him in the values appropriate to a ruler. The "gifts" presented to him at each station remind him of the qualities on which his stable and prosperous rule depend. In contrast to earlier "triumphs," Lydgate's poem moves toward a more significant allegorical structure and toward a greater exploitation of the verbal element of the pageant in its integration of scene and word, tableau and verse inscription. The poem draws together spectacle, allegory, and verbal gloss as it transmutes the impermanent occasion of the processional into a permanent artifact or word-painting of the event.

The experimental quality of the poem and the process of transmuting event into artifact appealed to Lydgate's immediate successors, who often found in his public and political poems the catalyst for their own experimentation. This influence, for example, is apparent in Dunbar's "To Aberdein," which incorporates features of Lydgate's "Triumphal" and skillfully extends them beyond their immediate limits.[21] Like Lydgate, Dunbar develops the poem as a word-painting of the occasion, representing the various scenes of the pageant that welcomed the queen to the city. But Dunbar goes even further than Lydgate in exploiting the verbal counterpart of the visual spectacle. In stanza 6, for example, he introduces a pattern of alliteration, internal echoing, and repetition in the echoing of "syne" and "ying," the first and last words of line 1, in the repetition of sounds in "quhyt," "browderit," and "rycht" in line 4, and in the play of "seimlie" and "besein" in line 7:

> Syne come thair four and tuentie madinis ying,
>   All claid in greine of mervelous bewtie,
> With hair detressit, as threidis of gold did hing,
>   With quyht hattis all browderit rycht brav[elie]
>   Playand on timberallis and syngand rycht sweitlie;
> That seimlie sort, in ordour weill besein,
>   Did meit the Quein, hir [saluand] reverentlie:
> Be blyth and blisfull, burcht of Aberdein.
> (ll. 41–48)

The result, in Dunbar's terminology, is an "anamalit" surface in which the poet's language transforms the occasional event, the substructure of the enamel, into a dazzling design of words and sounds that endures beyond the immediate moment of the event.

Similarly, Lydgate's "Ballade on a New Year's Gift of an Eagle, Presented to King Henry VI" served as a catalyst for Dunbar's "A New Year's Gift to the King."[22] Drawing together associations from classical mythology, biblical literature, and historical legend, Lydgate's poem amplifies the significance of the eagle to include the various gifts or qualities essential to the king—the blessings of Jupiter to whom the eagle is sacred, the peace represented by the olive the royal eagle brought to earth, and the "Honour of knighthoode, conquest and victorye"—and a similar array of gifts for the Queen Mother, Katherine. The double refrain, "Honour of knighthoode, conquest and victorye" (sts. 1–5) and "Helþe and welfare, ioye and prosparytee" (sts. 6–10), reinforces the dual emphasis of the two parts of the poem. In his poem, Dunbar distills into five perfectly crafted stanzas the qualities Lydgate catalogs at length. He shrewdly omits all narrative framework and allegorical devices, thus allowing the gifts themselves, the good fortune, prosperity, and peace he wishes the king, to stand in high relief.

Mummings and Public Spectacles

In several of the coronation poems, Lydgate is concerned with translating an event into a word-painting of the occasion. In his mummings, he moves a step closer to an actual tabloid, creating an interesting combination of speech and visual representation which had an impact on later drama. Some anticipation of his techniques in the mummings is found in the early pictorial poem, *Bycorne and Chichevache,* in which Lydgate's lines accompany a painted device hanging in the home of a wealthy citizen of London, and also in the didactic *Pageant of Knowledge,* a tabloid of the seven estates, the seven virtues of Sapience, the seven liberal arts, the seven planets, and the four seasons.[23] In both of these poems, Lydgate blends allegory, pageantry, commentary, and dramatic dialogue. In his seven mummings, he combines the forms of pictorial poem, masque, and tableau into dramatic "entertainments" designed to accompany dumb shows or pantomimes presented at the royal palaces or before civic audiences at banquets and other occasions. Although the poems were apparently written at different times, they share similar forms—the rhyme royal and the longer couplet form—and elevated styles.

The first of these pieces, the *Mumming at Eltham,* was written for the Christmas festivities of the king and queen at Eltham Palace in 1424.[24] In Lydgate's day, this palace, now in ruins, had a large banquet hall designed for theatrical performances. Located near Greenwich, it was a convenient stopping place for the royal entourage and a favorite residence of the three Henrys at Christmas time. *The Mumming at Eltham* begins with a description of the tableau, the appearance of Bacchus, Juno, and Ceres who bring presents of wine, wheat, and oil to the king. The next six stanzas expand upon the significance of these gifts in the manner of the "Ballade on a New Year's Gift" as symbols of peace, gladness, and plenty. But in contrast to the "Ballade," Lydgate develops the voice of the narrator more distinctly as a separate figure in this poem, who dramatically addresses the king and Queen Mother. Assuring them of peace, he reveals that Bacchus, Juno, and Ceres will drive Mars away.

The *Mumming of Bishopswood*[25] is considerably more innovative than the *Mumming at Eltham.* In this work, Lydgate combines the spring pageant and the conventional renewal of nature it represents with the political renewal of the state, a combination that is unique in the literature of the period. The poem, written for the "Shirreves of London," begins with the arrival of Flora, the daughter of spring, whom Lydgate represents clothing the earth and reviving the soil. The next three stanzas describe the influence of Flora on nature as she makes men, beasts, and birds rejoice. Stanzas 5–11 link the spring season with the end of the winter of adversity and the return of prosperity to all of the estates. Spring will bring the palm of victory to the prince, "noblesse in armes, lawde, honour, & glorie" to the knights, and peace to the people. Thus, the poet bids the audience rejoice.

The *Mumming at London,* performed before "þe gret estates of þis lande, þane being at London"[26] in 1427, turns from the gifts presented to the nature of the mythological figures themselves, developing the mumming into an elaborate allegory reminiscent of the descriptions of the gods in *Resoun and Sensuallyte.* Fortune, the "Lady of mutabilytee," first appears and, in a long speech, the narrator defines her characteristics, her dwelling place and its significance, and the men and women she has harmed. The second part of the mumming introduces four ladies who will protect men from Fortune's power—Prudence, Righteousness, Fortitude, and Temperance (the four cardinal virtues). Each lady is allegorized in elaborate detail in terms of her physical appearance, dress, and habits. The piece ends with the four goddesses uniting in song. Lydgate's tone in this presentation is more didactic and serious than it had been in the *Mumming at Bishopswood,* and the emphasis of the piece is more clearly on the moral lesson about the mutability of Fortune and the need to be virtuous to resist her. The poem probably served as an interlude in the festivities, followed by games and dances, and would have impressed the audience by its elevated style and decorum.

Lydgate's next two mummings, the *Mumming for the Mercers of London* and the *Mumming for the Goldsmiths of London,* were commissioned by burghers for a civic audience.[27] The *Mumming for the Mercers of London* was performed by the silk merchants' guild in honor of William Eastfield, the lord mayor of London, on Epiphany Eve, 6 January 1429. An even more densely packed tableau than the *Mumming at London,* the *Mumming for the Mercers* includes a dazzling array of allegorical figures and allusions in its first thirty-five lines. Presented as a letter from Jupiter to the mayor, the poem recounts the journey of Jove's messenger throughout the world to England to greet the mayor. As his letter is read aloud, the allegorical figures he refers to, a catalog of mythological and classical poets, appear and the speaker explains their names and importance. This device apparently delighted the bourgeois audience, including Shirley, who made numerous comments on the text in the margins of the manuscript. After the convocation of poets, the narrator traces Jove's journey with an abundance of geographical allusions. The climax of the piece occurs as Jupiter's messenger approaches London and sees a series of allegorical ships holding various characters who descend to greet the mayor.

The *Mumming for the Goldsmiths of London* forms a companion piece to the *Mumming for Mercers.* Performed for the same lord mayor about a month later, for the sacred feast of Candlemas (2 February 1429), the poem appropriately turns from the classical mythology of the earlier mumming to the biblical tradition. The narrator is Fortune, who presents King David, the model of the worthy king, "þe chaumpyoun / þat sloughe þe tyraunt, to gete him-self a prysse, / May to restore ageyne to Paradys" (ll. 12–14) and the twelve tribes of Israel. These figures bring the Ark of the Covenant to the city of London with its gifts of grace, good fortune, and prosperity and peace. Bidding the citizens of London defend this ark, the narrator envisions an era of peace and prosperity for the city. The two mummings, one humanistic, the other biblical, thus provide elaborate and richly allegorical tableaux in which the verbal representation approaches the boundaries of the visual.

The last two mummings, the *Mumming at Windsor* and the *Mumming at Hertford,*[28] again turn to royal audiences. According to Shirley, the *Mumming at Windsor* was a Christmas entertainment for King Henry VI, performed during his stay at Windsor Castle during 1429–30. Devised to show "howe þ'ampull and þe floure de lys came first to þe kynges of Fraunce by myrakle at Reynes," the mumming tells of the conversion of the French under King Clovis, an appropriate subject since Henry was about to leave for France to be crowned. With an occasional touch of humor reminiscent of the passages on women in the *Troy Book* and *Fall of Princes,* Lydgate describes how St. Clotilda, an example of the best of womanhood, brought the tokens of grace to Clovis:

> Hir hoolynesse Fraunce did enlumyne
> And Crystes fayth gretly magnefye.
> Loo what grace dooþh in wymmen shyne,
> Whas assuraunce noman may denye.
> To seye pleyne trouth nys no flaterye;
> But stabulnesse in wymmen for to fynde,
> Deemeþe youre selff wher it komeþe hem of kynde.
> (ll. 50–56)

These asides amused Shirley, who comments, "A daun Johan, est y vray?" The piece closes with a reminder that Henry VI is about to receive these tokens as he is anointed king of France. Presumably, Lydgate's description of the ampulla kept at Rheims, which would be used in the coronation ceremony, would call to mind the recent campaigns and capture of another French heroine, Joan of Arc, and the restoration of English rule.

The *Mumming at Hertford,* the last of these poems, is lighter in tone than the other mummings. Written at the request of John Brys, controller of the royal household, and performed for the king at Hertford Castle on Christmas, 1430, the poem presents the "rude uplandish people" complaining about their wives and the "boystous answere" of the wives in the satirical tradition of the *Wife of Bath's Tale* and Dunbar's "Tretis of the Twa Mariit Wemen and the Wedo." As the narrator explains to the king, the torment of married men is unbearable:

> For þey afferme þer is noon eorþely stryff
> May beo compared to wedding of a wyff,
> And who þat euer stondeþe in þe cas,
> He with his rebecke may sing ful offt ellas!
> (ll. 21–24)

As examples of his point, the six men come forward and offer their cases. Skillfully echoing the language of the Noah plays, popular lyric, and Chaucer's tales, especially the Clerk's envoy, the narrator describes how the wives manipulate, harangue, and emasculate their husbands. Robin the Reeve, for example, who complains that his wife, Beatrix Bittersweete, neither cooks for him nor looks after him, is afraid to speak up, for

Beautryce of him dooþe so sytel rekke,
þat with hir distaff she hitteþe him in þe nekke,
For a medecyne to chawf with his bloode;
With suche a metyerde she haþe shape him an hoode.
(ll. 51–54)

The wives echoing the archwife, Chaucer's Wife of Bath, protest that it is not the nature of wives to live silently and obediently and argue that they teach their husbands patience in order for them to reach heaven (ll. 168–72). The king cleverly evades ruling in the case for a year, granting the wives mastery until that time but warning men not to marry (ll. 246–54). Despite the preponderance of didactic and serious poems in his repertoire, Lydgate is effective in his foray into the satirical style in the *Mumming at Hertford,* and his treatment is original in its twist in the end.

In his public poems, Lydgate, is therefore politically conservative. The themes that tie these poems together—the qualities essential to a good ruler, the defense of Henry V's and Henry VI's right to the dual crown, and, above all, the desire for peace within England and externally with the European powers—reveal his role as a spokesman for the established order. But in his didactic emphasis on the responsibilities of a king or statesman and on the models the king inherits from the past, Lydgate tempers the official line, diplomatically directing the young Henry VI to goals that transcend the immediate Lancastrian political interest. His concerns are best summed up in the short poem, "A Praise of Peace," written soon after the death of Henry V.[29] In this poem, Lydgate extends the themes of the *Troy Book* epilogue and the *Siege of Thebes,* emphasizing the importance of peace above any other earthly ideal. Commenting on the three letters that make up the word "Pax," Lydgate links "polityk Prudence," "Auctorite," and "Xpus most digne of reverence" (Christ) to suggest the associations this word embodies. Peace, he stresses, is both the inward peace of conscience and the outward peace among people. It is the earthly version of the external peace God ultimately brings:

Pees is a vertu pacient and tretable,
  Set in quyet discoord of neihbours,
Froward cheerye pees makith amyable,
  Of throny roseers pees gradrith out the flours,
  Makith the swerd to ruste of conquerours

Provided by poeetys, nat slouh nor reklees,
And mediacioun of wise enbassitours,
The spere, maad blont, brouht in love and pees.
(ll. 49–56)

The remainder of the poem represents the initial establishment of peace on earth and the breach of peace beginning with Herod's slaughter of the innocents. From this violation descended other significant moments of strife, which Lydgate documents with numerous biblical, classical, and contemporary examples. The catalog ends with the recent wars between England and France, the victory of the recently deceased Henry V, and an earnest prayer for a return to peace.

By his poetic strategies in the political poems, Lydgate tempers the immediate demands of the events he considers. Experimenting in various ways with the occasional poem, he often turns the events or issues which underlie the poems into abstractions of more lasting significance. Stylistically, he achieves this effect in many poems by creating an intricate design of words and sounds, a dense poetic surface that corresponds to the *tableaux vivants* or pageants which graced official occasions. In his treatment, the occasional poem moves toward the realm of artifact, both in its transformation of mutable events into finely crafted structures and in its distillation of permanent values from impermanent events.

Chapter Six

The Poet of "Hie Sentence": Moral and Didactic Poems

Less ceremonious in style than the political poems, the group of approximately forty-five short moral and didactic poems and miscellaneous fables included in the Lydgate canon represent a neglected area of Lydgate's experimentation. Based on conventional subject matter, the poems range from straightforward ballades of practical advice, to gnomic reiteration of proverbial wisdom, to poignant and effective lyrics on the nature of man's position in the world. The recurrent themes of the moral poems—the transitoriness of the world, the limits of human vision, and the need for prudence, virtue, and good governance—strike a familiar note to the readers of late medieval poetry. But while Lydgate often begins with traditional themes and the popular ballade and fable forms, in many of the poems he manipulates his structures to achieve striking and innovative effects. Particularly in his treatment of the refrain poem, he introduces techniques that prompted poetic experimentation throughout the century. It is his combination of moral concern and poetic innovation that impressed contemporary critics, for example, Thomas Feylde, who sums up Lydgate's achievement by linking the "fruytefull and sentencyous" nature of his works and their rhetorical excellence, and Stephen Hawes, who praises Lydgate for "his faynynge with termes eloquent . . . Grounded on reasoun."[1]

"Little Homilies with Proverbial Refrains"

MacCracken's title in his edition of Lydgate's minor poems, "Little Homilies with Proverbial Refrains,"[2] covers a range of lyrics, some straightforward and uninspired moral poems, others of exceptional quality. Most of the poems are linked by a common eight-line stanza and the *a b a b b c b c* rhyme scheme associated with the ballade. All of the poems exploit the short proverbial refrain common in late medieval collections of lyrics like the Vernon MS to introduce, develop, and resolve their themes. Many of the lyrics share similar allusions and examples gleaned from classical sources, biblical stories, and contemporary history, and Lydgate often repeats his most effective images or examples with slight variation in several poems. The interest in these lyrics lies principally in the ways in which Lydgate manipulates his form to refurbish and revitalize his traditional matter.

A good example of his technique is provided by the lyric "Amor Vincit Omnia Mentiris Quod Pecunia" which introduces the series in MacCracken's collection.[3] This poem expands upon the Latin proverb that forms the title and the basis of its refrain, "Love is sette bakke, gold goth byfore, and mede." The opening stanza introduces the central conflict, "Whiche of the two by ust comparisoun / Love or money in valew doth excede?" (ll. 5–6). By means of carefully selected examples from classical literature, Lydgate dramatizes the precarious position of earthly love in the first thirteen stanzas. Although lovers profess to put all aside for love, the reverse is shown by old stories, for example, the legend of Troilus, the fate of Paris and Helen, Cleopatra and Antony, Alexander and Candace, and numerous others. Love and friendship are overthrown by gold and mede. In a stanza that stands out from the rest of the poem by its poignancy, Lydgate emphasizes the disappointing nature of earthly love by means of an effective seasonal image:

> Like to a tre, with fressh blosmes ladde,
> Which that in Aprill so lusti be and fayre;
> But whan in August folk[es] do repayre
> To gadre his fruyte, there is none found in dede:
> Of suche friendis there be mo than a payre,
> Save with fayre chiere they love nat but for mede.
> (ll. 99–104)

For true love and true mede, the poem concludes, man should turn to God.

By his manipulation of the refrain, Lydgate introduces a subtle play upon his familiar theme. In stanza 3, he shifts from the present "Love is sette bakke, gold goth byfore, and mede," to the past tense to suggest the continuity of the problem throughout human history. The change from "Love" to "Olde aqueyntaunce" in the refrain to stanza 5 ("Olde aqueyntaunce is set abakke for mede") enlarges the threat of "mede" to include not only physical love but also friendship. The alternation of these loves in the refrains to stanzas 6–9 culminates in the statement in the refrain to stanza 10 that "in eche court, gold goth before, and mede" and in stanza 13 that men "love nat but for mede." In the refrain to stanza 14, Lydgate turns from the notion of earthly "mede" to eternal reward to provide a new answer to his opening question. The final three refrains expand this vision of eternal "mede," concluding with a redefinition of the relation of love and reward that transcends the conflict of the opening stanza: "Suche love grounded in love and stablenesse / Shal have of God his gwerdoun and his mede."

Lydgate's modulation of his theme by means of subtle changes in the refrain and his use of crystallizing images and catalogs of examples are found in several of the lyrics with varying degrees of effectiveness. In both "A Froend at Neode" and "A Dity Upon Haste,"[4] he exploits the catalog of biblical and classical examples which he introduces in a more abbreviated and successful form in "Amor Vincit Omnia." In these poems, the device is attenuated and we almost lose sight of the points of the lyrics in the proliferation of examples. Both poems develop the effective seasonal imagery of "Amor Vincit Omnia" to emphasize the ephemeral nature of earthly experience. In "A Froend at Neode," the poet overhears a lark singing about the difficulty of finding lasting friendship: "þe worlde is divers, ffortune is chaungyng, / Ful weele is him þat fyndeþe a froende at neede." Turning from the spring opening of the first stanza to the image of the winter tree, he suggests the transitory nature of most men's friendships:

> Gret noumbre of frendes in prosperitee
> Whylest fortune shewiþe hir lookes glade;
> Gret prees of coustume is abowte þe tree,
> While þat boughes beon with fruytes lade;
> But whane þe braunches beon bareine and fade
> þat he revested is in wynters weede,
> Fare weele þe prees, þis likness þat I made,
> Is agayne hem þat fayle þaire freonde at neede.
> (ll. 9–16)

In "A Ditty upon Haste," Lydgate again modifies the seasonal image to provide an effective transition between two parts of the poem.

The opening stanzas enumerate the dangers of haste; the middle section of the poem offers a catalog of examples of these dangers; the last four stanzas introduce a different and beneficial kind of haste, haste toward God. In between the first two parts of the poem, Lydgate inserts an image of the changing seasons to suggest the futility of haste in the world by reminding the reader that each thing has its natural season (ll. 73–80). Finally, the two poems monitor their themes by skillful variations in the refrains.

Less effective in its exploitation of these devices is "Consulo Quisquis Eris"[5] which attempts, like "A Froend at Neode" and "A Ditty," to direct the reader from earthly to heavenly concerns. The first seven stanzas essentially advise the reader to follow the customs of the land—when in Rome do as the Romans do. The examples, however, are arranged randomly and do little to advance the author's case. Yet amid the scattered references are effective passages, particularly those in which Lydgate alludes adroitly to earlier texts. Warning us "among foxis be foxissh of nature," for example, he echoes a line from Chaucer's *Reeve's Tale,* "With empty hand men may noon haukys lure."[6] The line in Chaucer's text has an ironic resonance, and Lydgate's allusion adds a cynical note to the advice in the stanza. The conclusion of the poem, which suggests that we should reject the course of Alexander, Caesar, and Pompey and turn to God, is more loosely attached to the body of the lyric than the morals of "A Froend" and "A Ditty." The emphasis of the refrain on the relation of language to one's audience and the shift from decorous to virtuous language is reinforced only partially by the catalog and does not effectively anticipate the image of the perfect man, who has "no surfet in woord nor in language" (l. 104), and the interesting allusion to Pygmalion, the creator of life, and "quyknesse of language" (l. 112) with which the poem ends.

The theme of appropriate language which underlies "Consulo Quisquis Eris" recurs in several of the refrain poems. The lyric, "Say the Best, and Never Repent,"[7] develops the advice of its title in gnomic form, turning to the seven-line stanza and to shorter, pithier lines than the "Consulo." The technically intricate "Ballade" with which the poem opens contrasts sharply with the understated and sparse style of the "text." In the "Ballade," the stanzas are joined by recurrent rhymes; in the "text," each stanza is set off as a self-contained unit of proverbial advice. The poem concludes with the warning that the language of the world is full of doubleness. In "A

Wicked Tunge Wille Sey Amys,"[8] the most skillful of the lyrics on the theme of man's speech, Lydgate demonstrates the folly of attempting to avoid malicious speech by means of a humorous catalog. No matter what one's assets, wicked men will turn them into deficiencies:

> ȝif thow be sad and sowbre of contenaunce,
> Men will seyn thow thenkest somme tresoun;
> And ȝif thow be glad of daliaunce,
> Men wil deme it dissolucioun,
> Callen faire speche adulacioun
> ȝitte let hem speke & trist[e] right wel this,
> A wicked tonge wille alwey sey a-mys.
> (ll. 57–63)

Thus, he urges princes to avoid such men and seek a "gode tonge." Lydgate's strategy in this poem appears to have influenced Dunbar, who introduces a similar series of impossible situations in his lyric, "How Sall I Governe Me."[9] The poet complains:

> Giff I be lustye, galland and blythe,
> Than will thai say on me full swythe,
> Yon man out of his mynd is he,
> Or sum hes done him confort kythe.
> Lord God, how sould I governe me?
>
> Giff I be sorowfull and sad,
> Than will that say that I am mad;
> I do bot drowpe as I wald die,
> So will thai deyme baythe man and lad.
> Lord God, how sall I governe me?
> (ll. 6–15)

But Dunbar transforms the techniques he borrows from Lydgate to form a tighter and more effective poem. Shortening the length of his catalog and compressing the seven-line stanza to five, he places each example into sharp relief. In addition, Dunbar recasts Lydgate's stanzas as rhetorical questions which build up to the final stanza where the poet offers the answer in a new refrain, "The gratious God mot governe me" (l. 50).

Linked to the poems on appropriate language is one of Lydgate's most mysterious lyrics, "The Cok Hath Lowe Shoone,"[10] which emphasizes the wisdom of silence. Ultimately based on the *Disticha Catonis,* the poem recalls Chaucer's *Manciple's Tale* and the fables of the Cock and the Fox that underlie the *Nun's Priest's Tale.* But Lydgate's treatment is more cryptic than Chaucer's. Alluding to various proverbs and stories, he hints of profound truths hidden in the stanzas:

> The royall egle with his ffetherys dunne,
> Of nature so hih takith his flyght,
> No bakke of kynde may looke ageyn the sunne,
> Of ffrowardnesse yit wyl he ffleen be nyght,
> And quenche laumpys, though they brenne bright.
> Thynges contrarye may nevir accorde in oon,
> A fowle gloowerm in dirknesse shewith a lyght;
> Alle go we stille, the Cok hath lowe shoon.
> (ll. 41–48)

The poem finally has a hermetic quality. Lines recur mysteriously; many of the animal references remain veiled, and the poet resorts to a stance of silence at the end of the poem.

The remaining refrain poems focus primarily on two themes: just measure or good governance and the transitoriness of the world. Several of the lyrics, including "A Song of Just Mesure," "Mesure is Tresour," "Look into Thy Merour and Deeme Noon Othir Wight," and "Every Thing to his Semblable,"[11] emphasize the appropriate mean between extremes for man to follow on earth. "Mesure is Tresour" and "Every Thing to his Semblable" survey the various estates to suggest the benefits of true measure and the dangers of straying from man's position, while a "Song of Just Mesure" emphasizes the importance of moderation in worldly behavior. "Look in Thy Merour" advises men to govern themselves well before they judge others. "Every Thing to his Semblable" leads man through the world of likenesses and contraries and urges him to choose his true "semblable," God.

The vision of the world as a place of contraries and extremes is treated more dramatically in two of Lydgate's most effective refrain poems, "Ryme without Accord" and "Tyed with a Lyne."[12] These lyrics skillfully exploit their poetic form as an image of their themes. "Ryme without Accord" presents a world of contraries that may "ryme," that is, meet or appear together, but do not agree. Each stanza embodies these contraries, formally drawing them together in individual lines, in couplets, and in rhymes, but without resolving the oppositions they define:

> A myghti kyng, a pore regioun,
> An hasty hede, a comunalte nat wise,
> Mikel almes-dede and false extorcioun,
> Knyghtly manhod, and shameful cowardise,
> An hevenly hevene, a peyneful paradise,
> A chast doctryne with a false thought,
> First don on heede, and sithen witte to wise,
> It may wele ryme, but it accordith nought.
> (ll. 17–24)

The last stanza, with its change in refrain, beseeches God to deliver man from all contraries. In "Tyed with a Lyne," Lydgate lengthens the refrain and attempts to link it more significantly with the structural and syntactical pattern of the poem. In the first seven stanzas, he introduces an apparently insoluble problem: the narrator is caught at the midpoint of contraries represented by the stanza's balanced half lines:

> The more I go, the further I am behynde;
> The further behynde, the nere the weyes end;
> The more I seche, the wers can I fynd;
> The lighter leve, the lother for to wend;
> The lengger I serve, the more out of mynd. . . .
> (ll. 1–5)

The refrain syntactically echoes these contradictions and points to the wider implications of the narrator's plight: "Is this fortune, or is it infortune? / Though I go loose, I tyed am with a lyne." The remaining five stanzas define a way out of this quandary, a solution that is underscored by Lydgate's effective manipulation of the refrain. In stanza 8, the narrator concludes that "al the world stant in variaunce" amid the antitheses he has experienced, a conclusion underscored by Lydgate's first change in the refrain: "Late men dispute, whethir this be fortune? / No man so loose, but he is tied with a luyne (ll. 55–56). Again changing the refrain, in stanza 9 Lydgate warns against trusting false fortune that has brought about this instability. Stanzas 10–12 reveal that man must place his trust in God in order to be free of contraries.

The last category of refrain poems—on the transitoriness of the world—represent some of Lydgate's best secular lyrics. Many of these poems center around a single, effective image—the rose, the pilgrimage, the approach of Death—and by the manipulation of the image, give new life to essentially traditional matter. Two good examples of Lydgate's treatment are provided by the lyrics, "As a Mydsomer Rose" and "Timor Mortis Conturbat Me."[13] In "As a Mydsomer Rose," one of his most popular lyrics among his contemporaries, Lydgate combines many of the recurrent themes of his poetry into a superbly fashioned testament of the mutability of all earthly experience. The poem opens with the central image of the midsummer rose, at once a symbol of the variety, the beauty, and the fragility of man's life. As he examines more closely the nature of man's world in the next seven stanzas, Lydgate adds increased resonance to this image. God not only has made the world diverse, but also deceptive, like the beautiful flower with hidden thorns:

> Holsom in smellyng be the soote fflourys,
> Ful delitable outward to the sight;
> The thron is sharp, curyd with fressh colouris,
> Al is nat gold that outward shewith bright;
> A stokfyssh boon in dirknesse yevith a light,
> Twen ffair and foul, as God list dispoose,—
> A difference atuix[en] day and nyght,
> Al stant on chaunge, lyke a mydsomyr roose.
> (ll. 9–16)

Imminent in the earth's fairness and allure is its certain change. All things have brief favor; the various birds, for example, each hold our attention momentarily with their special note. But in this diversity is pain as well as pleasure. "The wolff of malys" tricks the innocent lamb. "Raveynours reigne, the innocent is bore doun, / Al stant on chaung, lyk a mydsomer roose" (ll. 39–40), now a symbol of vulnerability.

In the remaining seven stanzas, Lydgate introduces an *ubi sunt* catalog as a case in point. He poignantly evokes the powerful heroes and eloquent poets, who like the "mydsomer rose" ultimately faded. The last three stanzas of the catalog, however, give this familiar motif and his central image a new twist to provide an effective ending for the poem. Lydgate signals this change in stanza 13 by altering his refrain. Referring to the heroes as martyrs whose stories are "rad in metre and proose" (l. 102), he suggests that they are not forgotten, but "Ther goldene crowyns, maad in the heuenly stage, / Fressher than lilies, or ony somyr roose" (ll. 103–4). In stanza 14, Lydgate transforms the central image by distinguishing the martyred heroes' action, built on "rihtwisnesse," from the mutability of courtly things. "The whit lillye was ther chaast clennesse, / Ther bloody suffraunce was no somyr roose" (ll. 111–12). In the last stanza, he makes a final leap, linking the blood of these "martyrs" with Christ's wounds, the rose imprinted in our hearts:

> It was the Roose of the bloody feeld,
> Roose of *Iericho,* that greuh in Beedlem;
> The five Roosys portrayed in the sheeld,
> Splayed in the baneer at Ierusalem.
> The sonne was clips and dirk in euery rem
> Whan crist *Ihesu* five wellys lyst vncloose,
> Toward Paradys, callyd the rede strem,
> Off whos five woundys prent in your hert a roose.
> (ll. 113–120)

With this last expansion, the rose thus becomes a symbol not only of man's plight, but also of his salvation.

In "Timor Mortis Conturbat Me," Lydgate links the refrain, the catalog, and the central image of the chain of death. As the poem unfolds, the refrain takes on broader and broader meanings which are reinforced by the poet's continually expanding catalog. The lyric opens with a vision of the poet in bed, overcome with fear, as he thinks of man's condition. Man's trouble, he realizes, began with Adam whose disobedience brought him the fear of death. The catalog that follows provides a survey of human history from Adam through the Old and New Testaments and the famous secular heroes of the past who "were embracyed in the cheyne / Of *timor mortis conturbat me*" (ll. 87–88). Lydgate's technique in this poem again served as the catalyst for the experimentation of later poets, for example, Dunbar, who further integrates the refrain, catalog, and image of stalking death in his famous "Lament for the Makaris."[14]

In his manipulation of the refrain poem, Lydgate is linked to the late medieval poets of Digby MS. 102 and the Vernon MS who also treat the seven and eight line refrain stanzas in sophisticated ways. Like Lydgate, these poets turn to proverbial and moral refrains, subtly varying these refrains to develop their themes. Although they often effectively integrate refrain, form, and syntactical structure, Lydgate finally stands out from these late medieval poets in the systematic nature of his experimentation. The twenty-odd refrain poems represent a significant extension of their genre in their exploitation of a broad range of devices to develop the refrain, in their structural and syntactical experimentation, and in their treatment of dramatic images like the "somer Rose." Though not always poetically successful, Lydgate's innovations in these poems influenced such fifteenth- and early sixteenth-century writers as Dunbar, Henryson, Hawes, and Skelton.

Didactic and Satirical Poems

More straightforward than the refrain poems in their technique are the group of seven short didactic poems. Principally poems of practical advice, these lyrics translate into verse recommendations for diet, for appropriate table manners, and for the care and laundering of clothes. Their concerns suggest a broadening of the domain of poetry in English to include the subjects of the instructional manuals and courtesy books produced in the fifteenth and sixteenth centuries. Some of the poems, like "A Treatise for Lauandres" written for Lady Sibille Boys of Holm Hale in Norfolk, were commissioned by individual patrons. But the majority of the poems represent Lydgate's response to the practical concerns of his audience.

Two of these pieces, "Stans puer ad mensam," which survives in twenty-three manuscripts, and the "Dietary," which is extant in over fifty manuscripts, are among Lydgate's most popular poems. Indeed, they rank behind only the *Canterbury Tales, Piers Plowman,* and the *Prik of Conscience* in the number of surviving manuscripts. "Stans puer ad mensam," which advises young boys how to conduct themselves at the table, anticipates the lively advice of Polonius in Shakespeare's *Hamlet.* Thorough, almost to the point of ridiculousness, the speaker combines practical instruction with general advice:

> Who speketh tó the in ony maner plase,
> Lombysshly cast nat thyn hed adoun,
> But with sad cheer looke hym in fface;
> Walke demurely by stretys in toun,
> And advertyse of wisdam and resoun.
> With dyssolute langage thou do noon offence
> To-fore thy souereyn, while he is in presence.

> Pare clene þi nailles, thyn hondis wasshe also
> To-ffore mete, and whan thou doost aryse;
> Sitte in that place thou art assigned to. . . .
> (ll. 15–24)

The "Dietary," which survives in several versions, some with a brief "Doctrine for Pestilence," also mixes concrete recommendations about food, drink, and health with more general advice about moderate living. Crisp and polished in its style, the poem is an example of the instructional lyric in its most effective form. The carefully balanced lines of the stanzas ultimately take on a gnomic quality as Lydgate offers a prescription of healthful living for the reader:

> Thus in too thyngis stondith al the welthe
> Of sowle & bodi, who so list hem sewe,
> Moderat foods yeueth to man his helthe,
> And all surfetis doth fro hym remuewe,
> And charite to the sowle is dewe. . . .
> (ll. 161–65)

In contrast to the instructional poems, which encompass a broad range of topics, many of the satirical poems focus on a single subject, the duplicity of women. Some of the attacks are straightforward and familiar to readers of antifeminist literature. "Examples against Women,"[15] which falls into this category, is a brief anthology of biblical stories about the falsity of women from Eve to Delilah. The poet covers the expected ground, drawing from the pool of examples common to medieval authors with little new material. "The Pain and Sorrow of Evil Marriage" and "Beward of Doublenesse" also turn to the traditional antifeminist matter. But these poems take hints from Chaucer's *Wife of Bath's Tale,* the envoy to the *Clerk's Tale, The Merchant's Tale,* and the *Envoy to Bukton* to develop their subject in a fresh way. Echoing the Pardoner in his interruption of the *Wife of Bath's Tale,* the narrator of "The Pain and Sorrow of Evil Marriage" confesses that he was about to take a wife but fortunately was saved by friends from "Hell[e] gates" (l. 24). Expanding the ironic description of the Wife's prologue and the *Merchant's Tale,* he creates an amusing picture of the tribulations of marriage. Women, he complains, make marriage a continual purgatory:

Thus wedlok is an eldles penaunce,
  Husbondes knowe that haue experience,
A martirdome and a contynuaunce
  Of sorowe ay lastyng, a deedly violence,
  And this of wyves is gladly the sentence;
Vpon here husbondes when hem list be bold,
Howe they allone gouerne the howsold.

And if the husband happe for to thryve,
  She saith it is here prudent purviaunce;
If they go bak ageynward and vnthryve,
  She sayth it is his mysgouernaunce;
  He berith the wite of all such ordynaunce:
If they be poure and fall in[to] distresse,
She sayth it is his ffoly and his lewdnesse.
(ll. 64–77)

Anticipating the tone and imagery of Dunbar's famous "Tretis of the Twa Mariit Wemen and the Wedo," he likens women to various kinds of beasts, "vnstable / In ther desires" (ll. 92–93). The only solution is to avoid these "dredfull / peryllous / serpent[s]." The irony increases in "Beware of Doublenesse" as the speaker assumes the role of the advocate of women in an inconstant world. In carefully poised four-stress ballade stanzas, he turns the theme of many of the refrain poems, the variableness of the world, into a defense of the constancy of women, echoing Chaucer's envoy to the *Clerk's Tale.*

The "Ballade on an Ale-Seller"[16] is more cynical in tone than these lyrics. Spoken by a disillusioned suitor, the ballade paints a picture of women as mercenary, cunning, and deceptive. Using beauty as a lure, they tempt unsuspecting men and then make them pay dearly. Although the particular complaint is an old one, Lydgate gives it new vitality by means of the colloquial language of the speaker:

. . . yit ye be more slihe
  To make men put in you more affiaunce,
Your tresoure tenvoce, and for to sett vp hihe
  In eche of them ye putt withe desseyuaunce
  A garlek hed, and swer thus in substaunce—
"While the hed is hooli, withynne my chaplerie
I shal yow love, and moost in you affrye."
(ll. 15–21)

In his mixture of courtly complaint, antifeminist satire, and colloquial monologue, he anticipates Dunbar's and Skelton's ballades.

The range and versatility of Lydgate's low style is reflected in the remaining satiric poems "Horns Away," "A Ballade of Jak Hare" "Lydgate's Letter to Gloucester," "Ryght as Rammes Horne," and "So as the Crabbe Goth Forward."[17] "Horns Away" rebukes women for the elaborate horned headdresses that were fashionable in the early fifteenth century, suggesting that horns are for beasts, not beautiful women. Alluding to the Clerk's envoy, he warns wives to cast such inappropriate fashions away:

> Clerkys recorde, by gret auctoryte,
> Hornes were yove to bestys ffor dyffence—
> A thyng contrarie to ffemynyte,
> To be maad sturdy of resystence.
> But arche wives, egre in ther vyolence,
> Fers as tygre ffor to make affray,
> They haue despit, and ageyn concyence,
> Lyst nat of pryde, ther hornes cast away.
> (ll. 33–40)

In a typically Lydgatian gesture, he turns from the humorous images of the poem to a moral ending, advising women to emulate the Virgin Mary who wore only a kerchief on her head. Lydgate's audience apparently appreciated this twist, for according to manuscript evidence the poem was one of the most popular of the moral and satiric works in the fifteenth century. "Ryght as a Rammes Horne" and "So as the Crabbe Goth Forward" both exploit the refrain to undercut the attitudes of the stanzas. In "Ryght as a Rammes Horne," the stanzas provide a smug picture of perfection in the world while the refrain, "Conueyed by lyne—right as a rammes horne," casts doubt on this vision. As the lyric unfolds, the descriptions of perfection in the first lines of the stanzas become increasingly preposterous and the refrains become correspondingly ironic. The poem ends with a dubious vision of perfection. "So as the Crabbe Goth Forward," a free translation of a French poem, also paints a picture of an ideal world where there is no doubleness, but the refrain, "So as þe crabbe goþe forward," hints of the inaccuracy of this view. In the envoy, Lydgate sets things right as he warns princes that the opposite vision of the world is true. Duplicity has control and causes great disturbance in both France and England. A sign of this condition, he reveals in the final refrain, is "Howe þat þe crabbe gooþe backward!"

In his humorous "Letter to Gloucester," Lydgate develops the image of the ailing purse he borrows from Chaucer to seek remedy for indigency. While Chaucer substitutes the purse for the lady in his "Complaint" and plays upon the irony of the imagery transposed from one context to another, Lydgate both increases the humor by means of his image of the consumptive purse in need of a restorative and overplays his hand by attenuating the device. Borrowing from both Chaucer and Lydgate in "Sanct Salvatour! send silver sorrow,"[18] Dunbar restores the poem's levity by streamlining his stanzas, sharpening the wit, and refining the central image.

Fables

The fables represent a fourth major category of Lydgate's moral verse. Conceived as "dirk parables" or "wondirful liknessis" "vndir covert," these tales illustrate the medieval view of poetry as *fabula* or pleasing fiction that hides significant truth. Less overtly didactic than the refrain poems, the instructional lyrics, and the satires, the fables reveal another aspect of Lydgate's versatility as a moral poet. The term *fable* in the Middle Ages had a double meaning. Literally, it referred to tales with animal characters that were used as exempla to illustrate moral points. But *fable* also was the term employed to describe a tale that was fictitious or made up, in a broad sense, a pleasing surface that concealed an important truth. As Lydgate explains in the prologue to "The Churl and the Bird,"[19] fables are

> Problemys, liknessis & ffigures
>   Which previd been fructuous of sentence,
> And han auctoritees groundid on scriptures
>   Bi resemblaunces of notable apparence,
>   With moralites concludyng in prudence. . . .
>
> (ll. 1–5)

Again at the outset of *Isopes Fabules,* he argues that poets have hidden "notable sentence" under the familiar surfaces of their fictions (ll. 17–21). The role of the reader is to search out and prize this wisdom.

The seven *Isopes Fabules,* generally believed to be the earliest of Lydgate's fables, descended from a branch of the fable that was translated from Phaedrus' verse version into Latin prose by Romulus in the sixth century. Romulus's text, the source of the medieval Aesopic versions, was versified and amplified by an unknown "Walter" in the twelfth century and further expanded in the thirteenth century in the *Esopus Moralisatus.* Although it is not certain which text Lydgate used as his source, he appears to have based his tales on a Latin or a French version of the thirteenth century *Esopus.* Shirley's rubric in Ashmole MS. 59, which contains only the last of the *Fables,* links the tales with Lydgate and suggests that they were written while he was a student at Oxford.[20] Since Shirley's rubric refers only to one fable, it is possible that Lydgate composed the tales at different times and assembled the collection after the project was well under way. The first four fables, which adhere to the traditional order of the Aesop collections, are distinguished by their greater length and substance from the last three, which do not follow the scheme. In one manuscript, Trinity R.3.19, these two segments are separated from each other by unrelated texts.

In contrast to the ironic approach of Chaucer before him in the *Nun's Priest's Tale* and *Manciple's Tale* and to Henryson after him, Lydgate treats the Aesopic material in a fundamentally straightforward and didactic manner. He reduces the narrative material substantially and amplifies the moral passages so that the proportions of tale and commentary are reversed. The first two fables provide good examples of his emphasis. The opening tale of the Cock and the precious stone, which also introduces Henryson's collection, is an example of the value of diligence in Lydgate's version. Lydgate provides a long description of the Cock's appearance and his activities as keeper of the "tydes of þe nyght" and champion against sloth. The narrative itself is brief, occupying only three of the twenty stanzas. The bulk of the tale expounds upon the significance of the Cock's "dylygent trauayle" and the dangers of the vice of idleness. The concluding eight stanzas report the Cock's address to the jasp as he returns it to the dung heap where he found it. Although the jasp would delight a jeweler, the Cock reasons that the stone is of little use to him:

> Precyous stones longen to iewellers
> And to princes, when þey lyst wel be seyn:

> To me more deynte in bernes or garners
> A lytell rewarde of corn or good greyn.
> To take þys stone to me hit were but veyn:
> Set more store (I haue hit of nature)
> Among rude chaffe to shrape for my pasture.
> (ll. 169–75)

The envoy reiterates the importance of diligence and emphasizes the wisdom of the Cock's choice as a type of the virtuous man who avoids idleness and worldly riches. The theme of diligence thus ties together the various parts of the fable—description, narrative, and *moralitas*. In his "Taill of the Cok, and the Jasp," Henryson considerably changes Lydgate's interpretation.[21] By cutting out most of the opening description of the Cock, he places the emphasis squarely on his encounter with the Jasp and his rejection of the stone. The bulk of the tale in Henryson's version focuses on the elaborate rhetorical address of the Cock to the precious stone he abandons. The Cock's arguments that the stone is of little value to him are persuasive. But in the final two stanzas of the tale, Henryson undermines this position by a sudden shift in style and perspective. In restrained lines that provide a sharp contrast to the Cock's excessive rhetoric, he draws attention to the virtues of the stone the Cock has rejected:

> This iolie iasp hes properteis seuin:
> The first, of cullour it is meruelous,
> Part lyke the fyre, and part lyke to the heuin;
> It makis ane man stark and victorious;
> Preseruis als fra cacis perrillous;
> Quha hes this stane sall have gude hap to speid,
> Or fyre nor fallis him neidis not to dreid.
> (ll. 120–26)

The *moralitas* reinforces the view that the Cock has been misguided in passing up the stone that is "Mair excellent than ony eirthly thing." The Jasp represents "science" that is "eternall meit" to man's soul. Blinded by the Cock's rhetoric, the reader, too, has ignored the stone's value. As the narrator laments:

> Bot now, allace this iasp is tynt and hid.
> We seik it nocht, nor preis it for to find;

> Haif we richis, na better lyfe we bid,
> Of science thocht the saull be bair and blind.
> Of this mater to speik, I wair bot wind, . . .
> (ll. 155–59)

Concluding, he challenges us to seek the Jasp.

Lydgate's "Tale of the Wolf and the Lamb" serves as an example of the tyranny of the powerful. The fable opens with a vision of the world as a place of extremes—malice and innocence, fraud and truth, rancor and humble patience—with no sensible course in between. The great dominate and harrass the small. The story itself, which occupies only seven of the nineteen stanzas, is a case in point. A Wolf, who spies the unsuspecting Lamb drinking from a stream, rebukes him for befouling his water as he claims the Lamb's father had done before him. In a lively dialogue, the Lamb defends himself, arguing that the Wolf's accusation is unfounded since he stands downstream. The truth is clear, but the Wolf ends the discussion by devouring the Lamb. The poet ironically notes the Wolf's last words to the Lamb, "The laws shall part vs, whyche of vs haþ ryght" (l. 292), and adds, "But he no lenger on þe lawe abood, / Deuouryd þe lambe & aftyr soke hys blood" (ll. 293–94). The remainder of the fable emphasizes the greater value of the Lamb than the Wolf to man and demands what justice a poor man can expect from the law while the conclusion suggests that men will get their just desserts only after death. Again, Henryson directs the focus of the fable away from the obvious moral to a more complex concern. By stripping away the commentary and amplifying the debate between the Wolf and the Lamb, Henryson increases our sympathy for the innocent Lamb. Introducing the language of legal statutes in the Lamb's arguments, Henryson accentuates both the Wolf's fundamental violation of justice and the ineffectiveness of man's law. Without the heavy-handed moralizing of Lydgate's tale, Henryson thus develops a scathing and more troubling commentary on the suffering of the innocent and the miscarriage of justice in the world.

These two examples reveal the two poets' considerable differences as fabulists. Lydgate's main interest is in the underlying moral of the narrative, which he accentuates by his didactic frame and digressions. All of the other elements of the fable—the animal characters, the plot, the dialogues, the narrative commentary—are directed to the didactic concern. Thus, Lydgate typically reduces the narrative episodes to a small proportion of the tale and expands the frame segments, the portions of commentary, from his sources. Similarly, his characters often speak with the moralist's voice and are developed only briefly as appendages to the plot. Henryson envisions a more problematical world than Lydgate does in which the "blind beast" of the fable, a type of the imprudent man in the world, has difficulty in distinguishing truth from falsehood, friend from foe, the "feyneid language sweit" of poetry from the false rhetoric of flattery. His characters, fully developed in their own right, often cloud or complicate with their speeches and actions the original straightforward morals of the sources. We are left with an uncertain relation of tale and *moralitas,* and the poet finally hides in silence at the end of the collection. The world of the *Fabillis* is troubling; man's only resource is prudence; and the poet's role is to document the pitfalls and dilemmas of the "blind" man in the world rather than to provide clear moral solutions.

Although Lydgate's three non-Aesopic fables—*The Churl and the Bird, The Debate of the Horse, Goose, and Sheep,* and *Fabula duorum mercatorum*—reveal a similar concern with the moral impact of the story, they present their matter in a more artistically skillful fashion than the early fables.[22] *The Churl and the Bird,* a translation from a French tale, probably a version of the story told in the *Disciplina Clericalis* of Petrus Alfonsus, is a thoroughly effective performance. The poem, which was popular in the fifteenth century and circulated in several Chaucerian anthologies, recounts the story of an impressive song bird who is trapped by a Churl and locked in a cage. Echoing Chaucer's *Manciple's Tale,* the Bird insists that she cannot sing if she is not free:

> And thouh my cage forged were of gold,
> And the pynaclis of berel & cristall,
> I remembre a prouerbe seid of old,
> 'Who lesith his fredam, in soth, he lesith all. . . .
> (ll. 92–95)

She persuades the Churl that if he frees her, she will give him three important pieces of wisdom. He agrees, and after warning man of hidden perils, the bird advises the Churl first not to be too credulous, second not to desire the impossible, and third not to regret the past. Having escaped, the Bird taunts the Churl for foolishly letting her go, revealing that she had a stone of magical properties in her body. The Churl laments his loss only to have the Bird reprimand him for ignoring her advice.

The fable contains an effective balance between narrative and didactic elements. Lydgate skillfully draws his characters, making the Churl not only dull witted, but proud, greedy, and domineering. Initially, the Churl covets the Bird, not for the beauty of its song, a motive in some of the other versions, but to dress up his garden, an object of his attention and pride (ll. 45–47). The Churl boorishly thinks of eating the Bird when it will not sing, but the Bird persuades the Churl that there will be too little meat on her body to be worth the effort. Playing up the Bird's wit, Lydgate amplifies her dialogue, sprinkling it with Chaucerian and proverbial allusions. He also accentuates her moment of revenge as she reduces the Churl to tears once she is free by revealing how she has tricked him. With considerable disdain, she patronizes her captor:

> To heeryn a wisdam thyn eris ben half deeff,
> Lik an asse that liseth on a harpe,
> Thou maist go pypen in a ivy leeff;
> Bett is to me to syngyn on thornes sharpe,
> Than in a cage, with a cherl to karpe. . . .
> (ll. 274–78)

The points of moral wisdom, which Lydgate repeatedly works into the tale to clarify and amplify the didactic potential of the story, are palatable in context.

The *Debate of the Horse, Goose, and Sheep,* written shortly after 1436, the year of the duke of Burgundy's attack on Calais to which the poem alludes (l. 413), develops the traditional debate among animal characters familiar in English literature in *The Owl and the Nightingale* and Chaucer's *Parliament of Fowls*. Lydgate's tale, which was popular among his contemporaries, plays upon the ingenuity and idiosyncratic wit of the three animals as each vies to be judged the most useful to man. The Horse intelligently alludes to his renowned ancestors who have aided worthy knights—Alexander's Bucephalus, Hector's Galathe, Perseus' Pegasus, "the hors of Fame," the magical horse of the *Squire's Tale,* and Zechariah's four diversely colored steeds—and then enumerates his many roles in everyday life. The Goose, more down to earth in her approach, assures the judges that every part of her body has some purpose for man. Goose grease provides remedy for gout, the quills provide pens, the feathers serve in arrows, the down is for pillows, while the turds, unlike horse dung, are good for burns. She concludes by emphasizing the necessity of her arrows for war, advising the audience of her role in victories from Roman times to the capture of the French king at Poitiers. The Sheep, too meek to speak for herself, reminds the judges through her interloquitor, the Ram, of the value of her wool in English trade and, more importantly, of her associations with Christ and the cause of peace, clinching her argument by demanding whether they prefer peace or war. The debate degenerates as the animals refute their claims and the judges determine that all three are useful to the state. The concluding stanza of the tale and the envoy contain Lydgate's didactic flourish as he emphasizes the moral underpinning of the story by his refrain: "No man shuld of hih nor lowe degre, / For no prerogatiff his neihbore despise." But, in contrast to the skillful counterpointing of story and moral commentary in the tale, the didacticism of the envoy gets the better of Lydgate and he ends by obscuring his point in his profusion of moral commentary.

The *Fabula duorum mercatorum,* the last of the three non-Aesopic fables, amplifies and elevates rhetorically a straightforward exemplum from the *Disciplina Clericalis.* In its simple form, the tale narrates the adventures of two merchants, close friends, whose friendship is tested. One friend gives up his bride for the other, while the second man takes the blame for a murder he did not commit to rescue his friend. Lydgate significantly amplifies this simple framework both to make it more stylistically decorous and to extract its full moral import. Imitating Chaucer's *Man of Law's Tale,* he adds numerous rhetorical digressions—on the geography of Egypt (ll. 134 ff.), on the nature of love and friendship (ll. 161 ff.), on the bitterness of absence (l. 420), on the changeability of Fortune (ll. 549, 666 ff.), and on the virtue of patience (ll. 589 ff.), as well as three lengthy and elaborate complaints: the poet's lament that his style is unworthy of his task of conveying the merchant's sorrow, the grief-stricken merchant's complaint (ll. 549 ff.), and the prayer of the actual murderer, overcome with guilt (ll. 792 ff.). These passages are drawn with a precision of language and a variety of figures that later poets often found worthy of imitation. But more important, Lydgate's rhetorical passages, like Chaucer's in the *Man of Law's Tale,* emotionalize the action and give the simple plot a new intensity. As in the *Troy Book,* the digressions magnify the characters' sense of loss and their dilemmas in an uncertain and transitory world. With the stylistic performance of this tale, we come full circle from the simple moral commentary of Lydgate's early Aesopian fables.

In assessing Lydgate's importance as a moral and didactic poet, one is impressed by the range and variety of his efforts. In the short lyric form, he experiments with many of the familiar types—the moral ballade, the refrain poem, the instructional poem, the gnomic lyric, the moral satire, and the reflective lyric. In each category, Lydgate explores the limits of the form, in some cases by amplifying an existing image or motif or reassembling traditional elements, in others by technically developing an organizing structure, a device, or a refrain. His attempt both to expand the boundaries of the didactic lyric in English to include new matter and purposes and to extend the traditional forms impressed contemporaries. Although his innovations as a didactic poet produced only mixed success, they often led to more effective experimentation with the moral ballade, the refrain poem, the instructional lyric, and the fable by the English and Scottish poets—Henryson, Dunbar, Hawes, and Skelton—who tacitly acknowledged Lydgate as one of their "maisters."

Chapter Seven

Religious Poems: Saints' Lives, Lyrics, *The Life of Our Lady*

The body of religious poetry attributed to Lydgate, which contains instructional poems, translations of hymns and psalms, prayers, poems on the passion, Marian lyrics, saints' lives, and religious narratives, represents one of his most significant contributions as an English poet. In these works, written at various stages in his career, Lydgate presents himself as a poet who attempts to break new ground as a religious writer. In his prologue and in many of his lyrics, he suggests that he seeks to create a new medium and form in English worthy of the noble role he envisions for the religious poet. Underlying the diversity of these poems is a marked concern with the literary rather than the didactic or devotional value of the verse, a tendency that becomes a prominent feature of the fifteenth-century religious lyric.[1] This emphasis finds form in two aspects of Lydgate's style, in the tendency toward extreme amplification and in the development of an elevated aureate style. The effect of these techniques is to impress the reader with the magnitude of the poet's subject matter and move him toward awe and admiration for the object or event the poem celebrates.

In several of the religious poems, Lydgate draws attention to his effort to create a new poetic mode in English. Two examples, the psalm "Misericordias Domini in Eternum Cantabo" and the Marian lyric "The Ballade at the Reverence of Our Lady Qwene of Mercy," illustrate his redefinition of his medium as a religious poet.[2] Both poems provide statements of his ideal of the religious lyric and impressive examples of its fulfillment. The "Misericordias Domini" defines the style and purpose of the religious lyric by means of a contrast between sacred song and all other types of poetry. In its emphasis on song and poetry rather than on God's mercies, Lydgate's version of the psalm differs from most other renditions. The first stanza of the poem announces Lydgate's purpose, the true purpose of all lyric, the glorification of God:

> Alle goostly songis & ympnes that be songe,
>   Of Oold and newe remebrid in scripture,
> Hevenly symball or bellis that be ronge,
>   To preyse the lord, by musyk or mesure,
>   Fynal intent of euery creature
> Shulde resounne to Goddys hih preysyng,
>   For which, o Lord! whil that my lyff may dure,
> Eternally thy mercies I shal syng.
>
> (ll. 1–8)

Stanzas 2–4 introduce a model of this type of song, the hymns of the poet-king David, who "with his harpe sang solempnely" the holy song of "Misericordias domini."

The next eight stanzas review the types of secular song which the poet put aside in order to sing of God's praise:

> Ther be Canticulis of Conquest and victorye
>   That be songe at feestis marcial,
> And ther be songis of palmys transitorye,
>   With corious meetrys that be *poetical;*
>   Laureat tryvmphes, proud and Imperial,
> With boosty blowe in charys cleer shynyng,
>   Al this left off, with voys memoryal,
> Eternally thy Mercies I shal syng.
>
> (ll. 33–40)

As he moves from the epic poems of Virgil, Dictys, Dares, and Lucan and the great medieval stories of Alexander, Troy, and Thebes, to the false allurements and "feynyng" of Circe and the Sirens, Lydgate's vision of secular song becomes increasingly debased.

The remaining stanzas turn by contrast to the sacred canticles of God's followers and reverse the direction of the first twelve stanzas by working their way from the low point of the Sirens' song to a magnificent example of the highest form of lyric, the sacred song, in his concluding hymn. By a change in style and technique, Lydgate distinguishes this section from the first half of the poem. Repeatedly inserting Latin refrains from the canticles to illustrate the sacred songs he describes, he creates in this section an atmosphere of celebration distinctly different from the first twelve stanzas. The frequency and intensity of the refrains mount as we reach the final stanza, the climactic example of true song.

In the opening stanzas of the "Ballade at the Reverence of Our Lady Qwene of Mercy," Lydgate provides a similar definition of the role of the religious poet. Echoing the *Troilus* narrator's concluding admonition, he rejects the style of "olde poets," the poets of love:

> A thowsand storiis kowde I mo reherse
> Off olde poetis, touchynge this matere,
> How that Cupide the hertis gan to perse
> Off his seruantis, settyng tham affere;
> Lo, here the fin of the errour and the werre!
> Lo, here of loue the guerdoun and greuaunce
> That euyr with woo his seruauntis doth avaunce!
> (ll. 1–7)

As in the "misericordias Domini," Lydgate announces his intention to "redress" or reform his style to develop a new kind of poetic "song." In stanzas 2 and 3, he indicates that he seeks a medium capable of expressing his unsurpassed praise of Mary: "I wil now pleynly my stile redresse, / Of on to speke at nede that will not faile" (ll. 8–9).

The body of the poem provides the response to Lydgate's plea, a celebration of the Virgin in a style distinct from that of the "olde poets" of stanza 1. Lydgate repeatedly extends the Latin rhetorical traditions in which he works to create a medium that is more dazzling than any before him. His technique is to amass striking images, allusions, and epithets, to overwhelm the reader by unusual coinages, elaborate aureation, and exploitation of internal rhymes, alliterations, and meter and thus move him to awe and admiration. While he combines many of the traditional images of Mary in his tribute—the star of stars, the jewel, the enclosed garden, the healing balm, the flower of flowers—he presents these images in such rapid succession and with such an elaboration of stylistic and linguistic devices that the overall effect is quite different from the passage of Alanus's *Anticlaudianus,* his immediate source.[3] The first stanza, with its elaborate imagery, alliteration, repetition, and intricate pattern of sounds, is typical of his treatment:

O sterne of sternys with thi stremys clere,
  Sterne of the see, [on]-to shipmen lyght and gyde,
O lusty lemand, moost plesaunt to appere,
Whos bright bemys the clowdis may not hide,
O way of lyfe to hem þat goo or ride,
  Haven aftyr tempest surrest as to ryve,
    On me haue mercy for thi Ioyes fyve.
(ll. 22–28)

In both poems, Lydgate thus indicates that the medium of the religious poem stands apart from other types of "song." Its style is directed to the praise of God, and the poet who would undertake this mission must strive to "redresse," reform, and refine his craft.

Instructional Poems

Even among the most commonplace of the religious poems, the poems designed to instruct the laity in the basic concerns of the Christian faith, Lydgate's effort to "redresse" his medium as a religious poet is apparent. These poems, vernacular renditions of the Paternoster, the ten commandments, the articles of the Creed, the seven sacraments, the seven works of mercy, the seven cardinal virtues, and the seven deadly sins, were written for the lower clergy and, in some cases, the laity, to help them teach and learn effectively the essential tenets of Christian worship. In the fourteenth and early fifteenth centuries, this kind of instruction became extremely popular and many writers expressed their concern that the articles of the faith be equally accessible in English as in other languages. The author of the Vernon MS, which contains several instructional poems in English, makes this ambition clear:

Lewed men be not lered in lore,
As clerkes ben in holi writ;
þauȝ men prechen hem bifore,
Hit wol not wonen in heore wit
. . . .
þerfore ichave on Englisch wrouȝt.[4]

Technically, a number of Lydgate's religious poems fall into the category of simple instructional poems, including "The Pater Noster Translated," a seven-stanza exposition of the petitions of the Paternoster; "The Virtues of the Mass," a reminder to priests of their appropriate role in the Mass; "The Fiftene Tokyns Aforn the Doom," a description of the fifteen signs of Doomsday; and "A Kalendare," a review of the festivals of the Church year.[5] But even these simple poems show a more literary treatment than their counterparts in the fifteenth-century collections. In his poem on "The Pater Noster Translated," for example, Lydgate turns to the formal ballade stanza to clarify and skillfully amplify each phrasal unit of the Paternoster. The overall effect of the poem is artful and impressive, especially when set beside the other surviving fifteenth-century versions, for example, those collected in Brown's *Religious Lyrics of the 15th Century.*

In a second poem on the Paternoster, Lydgate experiments on a more ambitious scale with the familiar form.[6] The poem is obviously directed to a sophisticated and literate reader who would appreciate the extraordinary embellishment of this prayer, rather than to a lower-class audience. Lydgate divides the poem into five parts which he systematically amplifies. The first three stanzas, the narrator's introduction, raise the problem of finding a medium suitable for divine praise in an artful variation of the humility topos. In the second section, stanzas 4–10, the narrator announces his subject, Christ's teaching of the Paternoster, and suggests that four virtues in particular belong to prayer, and above all, to the Paternoster, "crowned among praieris" (l. 31). In a tour de force of amplification designed to build up the significance of these four things, Lydgate recalls all of the important fours which the value of this prayer surpasses:

> I speke of foure, first in myn avys,
>   Nat of the foure hevenly Gospelerys;
> Nor of foure floodys that came fro paradys
>   That norisshe al Egypt with ther fressh Reverys;
>   Nor how Ezechiel with his ffour speerys
> Callid Quatour rote wich in al vertu schyne;
>   But of a mater longyng to prayeerys
> Tauht by Iesu, our rudenesse tenlumyne.
>
> I nat remember of the foure Elementys,
>   Nor of the four sesouns of the yeer,
> Of foure complexiouns dyuerse of ententys,
>   Of sonne or mone, why they be dirk or clee;
>   Nor of foure wyndys wich dyuersly appeer. . . .
> (ll. 41–53)

Lydgate's amplification in each section becomes increasingly elaborate as if he were trying to outdo his own effort. The third part, stanzas 13–17, expands upon the meaning of the terms "pater" and "noster," brilliantly drawing out all of the implications of these words. The fourth section, the longest and most splendid of the poem (sts. 18–38), provides an exposition of the prayer almost three times as long as the amplification of "The Pater Noster Translated." In these stanzas, Lydgate stretches each phrase of the prayer to its limits and extends, insofar as possible within the bounds of language, its meaning and effect. "Give us thy daily bread," for example, becomes in Lydgate's version a skillfully extended passage of thirty-two lines.

The literary emphasis and particularly the interest in elaborate amplification also characterize several pieces which appear to have been commissioned for private use. Two poems, "The Virtues of the Mass" and the "Procession of Corpus Christi,"[7] illustrate the range of the sustained amplificatory mode Lydgate develops in the instructional poems. In "The Virtues of the Mass," written for the pious countess of Suffolk, Lydgate interprets the meaning of each part of the Mass, alternating the Latin text with extended amplification of its significance. Superimposed upon this process of amplification is a second kind of amplification in which Lydgate structurally extends the sequence of the Mass which forms the center of his poem. Within the traditional sequence between the *Sanctus* and the *Agnes Dei,* for example, he inserts his own prayer to the sacrament (ll. 321–92), itself a prelude to the paraphrase of the Lord's Prayer that follows. At the beginning of the description of the Mass, he further amplifies by adding a translation of Psalm 42, *Judica me deus* (ll. 89–114), and at the end two digressions that contain St. Bernard's and St. Augustine's views on the Mass. In two manuscripts, this performance is in turn framed by a further amplification in two short pieces placed at the beginning and end of the *Virtues of the Mass,* an introductory "Exortacioun to Prestys when they shall say theyr Masse," and a concluding "On Kissing at *Verbum caro factum est,*" a brief explanation of why one kneels in church to kiss stone, earth, wood, and iron.[8] The final effect is a continually expanding perspective on the traditional ceremony of the Mass.

In the "Procession of Corpus Christi," Lydgate amplifies the significance of the procession at the great annual festival of Corpus

Christi in London in which the sacraments were carried through the streets by members of the furriers' guild.[9] In contrast to his treatment in some of the secular pageant poems, Lydgate does not amplify the externals of the procession in this poem. Rather, he elaborates upon the meaning of the Corpus Christi itself. With an abundance of learned detail, he moves back in time to antecedents of the Communion in the Old Testament—Adam and the Tree of Life, Melchisedoch offering bread and wine, Abraham offering bread, Isaac's seed, Jacob's ladder, Moses and the manna that fed the Israelites, Aaron, David, Isaiah with his vision of vines—drawing out each example. From the Old Testament scenes, he turns to the examples from the New Testament and from the church fathers, and concludes by urging us to revere the sacrament. Although the main structure of the poem was determined by the order of the pageants of the actual procession, Lydgate's amplification underscores the resonance of the sacrament's significance throughout history in its various prefigurations and links together associations not immediately elicited by the visual representation.

A similar propensity to amplify underlies the long instructional poem commonly attributed to Lydgate,[10] the translation of Guillaume de Deguileville's *Pélerinage de la Vie Humaine.* Deguileville, a Cistercian monk at the abbey of Chalis in the early fourteenth century, composed a trilogy describing man's pilgrimage through the earthly life in the *Pélerinage de la Vie Humaine,* the passage of his soul after death to Salvation in the *Pélerinage de l'Ame,* and the exemplary life and death of Christ in the *Pélerinage de Jésus Christ.*[11] These poems, written without the knowledge of Dante's *Comedia,* define the struggle between the forces of good and evil for the soul. Deguileville's works had considerable popularity in the fifteenth century, and Lydgate's translation, commissioned by Thomas Montachute, the second husband of Alice Chaucer, was one of several prepared during this period.

Lydgate's account, based on Deguileville's second and somewhat amplified version, begins with an original prologue, a translation of the author's prologue, and a vision of the Holy City of Jerusalem which prompted the author to undertake a pilgrimage. In the house of Grace Dieu, the narrator is instructed in the dogmas and sacraments of the church and is given advice by Reason on the conduct of his pilgrimage. Lengthy discourses follow between Nature and Grace Dieu and between Aristotle and Sapience on the eucharist before Grace Dieu equips the narrator with allegorical armor for his pilgrimage. At the beginning of his journey, the narrator encounters Rude Entendement (Ignorance), who is defeated by Reason, and Youth, who, at the first crossroad leads him away from Labor and toward Idleness. The pilgrim then meets various sins—Gluttony, Sloth, Pride, Envy, Wrath, Tribulation, Avarice, Heresy—against whom he must defend himself. Satan blocks his path, and the narrator is forced to swim across the sea to escape him and the whirling tower of worldly Pleasure. Finally, Grace Dieu sends the Ship of Religion to save him. The narrator chooses the Cistercian castle, where he meets Obedience, Abstinence, Chastity, Poverty, and Prayer and learns about the abuses within the church. After the castle is attacked by Detraction, Treason, and Envy and defended, Age and Sickness warn the narrator of Death's approach. The narrator prays to God before he finally awakens.

Although Lydgate's version extends Deguileville's 18,123 lines to 24,832, he adds little of significance. Most of his amplification is either padding or gloss—circumlocutions, tags, reduplication of expression, didactic digressions, and etymologies. Contrary to his practice in his secular long poems, he makes no major revision or redirection of emphasis, nor does he make a significant effort to elevate the action stylistically. The allegory remains fairly literal, dependent on intellectual correspondences rather than imaginative associations or visual suggestions. The result is a diminishing rather than an extension of the allegory. In a sustained form, the amplificatory techniques of the short instructional lyric are of limited effectiveness.

Translations of Psalms and Hymns

In his paraphrases of psalms and hymns, Lydgate is primarily concerned with creating artistic versions of his texts. His translations were probably intended for private use since, in the fifteenth century, the service, except for the sermon, was delivered in Latin. Lydgate's poems, which range from simple paraphrases to intricate and ambitious renditions loosely joined to the original, served to illuminate the Latin text and make it more elaborate and meaningful. The most straightforward of the pieces, *Benedic Anima Mea,* a translation of Psalm 102, was written for Edmund Lacy, dean of the chapel at Windsor, according to the rubric in Trinity MS. R.3.20, fol. 165, "whyles þe kynge was at evensonge."[12] This piece devotes a stanza to each verse of the psalm, gracefully embellishing the original. In *Deus in nomine tuo salvum me fac* (Psalm 53) and in the later *De profundus* (Psalm 129), Lydgate develops his techniques of amplification, reduplication of expression, verbal echoing, and alliteration to produce more independent and elaborate versions.[13] This tendency is merely incipient in the translation of Psalm 53, which renders some verses closely but considerably embellishes the end of the psalm, expanding the *Gloria* and the *Sicut erat* to one stanza each. The *De profundis,* Lydgate reveals, was written in his old age at the request of Abbot Curteys (ll. 161–68). In an expansive introductory section he explains why the psalm is said especially for Souls in Purgatory, interpreting the text through the prefigurations of Jonah, Daniel, Joseph, Sampson, and the three children in the fire, and the readings of Augustine, Jerome, and David. The body of the poem contains the paraphrase itself with each stanza rendering a verse of the psalm. Finally, he adds a personal conclusion which further stretches out his material. The overall effect is a considerably inflated piece in which the digressive frame overshadows the impact of the central text.

The potential of Lydgate's literary adaptations of the Psalms and hymns is best realized in the paraphrase of the hymn *Te Deum Laudamus,* initially attributed to Ambrose, but later assigned to Nicetas, bishop of Remesiana.[14] In addition to the techniques of amplification, verbal echoing, and alliteration characteristic of the other translations, Lydgate experiments effectively with language, introducing a striking combination of English and Latin that moves beyond the language of religious praise in English before his time.[15] Some anticipation of his techniques is found in the translations of the Ambrosian hymn *Criste qui lux est et dies,* and the Passion hymn *Vexilla regis prodeunt* by Venantius Fortunatus.[16] In both of these works, Lydgate exploits the verse of the original to form a kind of "macaronic" poem, in the first case by using the first line of each verse in Latin as the last line of each stanza, in the second, by interweaving lines 3 and 4 of the Latin verse as lines 6 and 8 of his ballade stanza. In the *Vexilla regis,* he also begins to interchange Latin and English expressions, creating a lofty and elevated effect.

The manipulation of language is considerably more ambitious in *Te Deum Laudamus.* One of the most popular nonbiblical hymns, this poem was translated several times in Old and Middle English.

Lydgate's version, however, stands out from the other translations in its fusion of English and Latin to create a medium of religious praise. In the first stanza, Lydgate exploits the techniques of the macaronic lyric, alternating Latin phrases from the hymn with English amplification and reinforcing the effect with prominent alliteration and echoing. His language in this stanza only occasionally borders on the aureate, for example, in the line "O ffemynyn fadir funte and foundoure" (l. 5). As the poem proceeds, however, Lydgate's English and Latin begin to merge, causing the reader to overlook the normal bounds of each language. Stanza 2, for example, contains the line "tibi coriously cantant celi celorum" (l. 11) worked in between lines of alternating English and Latin. Many of the lines of stanza 3 develop an even more intricate relation between the English and Latin sounds and meanings. For example, line 17, "*Pleni sunt celi* with plentevousnesse," exploits the connotations of root and stem to enrich the meaning of each, while in line 23, "O Infynyt fontayn ful of felicite!," the echoing expands the significance of the word "fontayn." In stanzas 4 and 5, the wordplay becomes even more extreme in lines like "*Te Chorus* glorious of apostolate, / Memorial make, modulacioun, / The laudable nombre of the prophetys astate / Evir loyng gaudent in Iubilacioun, / Te letabilem laudat in laudacioun . . ." (ll. 25–29).

In the second half of the poem, stanzas 6–13, Lydgate tempers his language as the narrator addresses Christ directly and prays for his mercy:

> Deere lord of thyn digne excellence,
>   This day conserve us from confusioun,
> The which is synne, slouth, and necligence;
>   Haue mercy on us, and make an vnyoun
>   Lat *misericord* discend from thy domynyoun
> *Miserere nostri* lord, as thu art gracious,
>   And put us not in-to perpetual prisoun,
> *Te laudat omnis spiritus.*
>
> (ll. 81–88)

The simple style of this section forms an effective contrast with the opening five stanzas, reinforcing the dual emphasis of the poem—God's awesome splendor and his limitless kindness to man. By his manipulation of language in this poem, Lydgate thus creates a

medium uniquely suited to his purpose and ac...
had not been produced in English before him.

Prayers to Saints

Lydgate's fourteen verse prayers to saints, generally judged to be the least interesting of his religious lyrics, experiment with mixed success with the elevated style of praise of the translations. Many of the prayers were composed for use in divine service at the request of noble patrons. One of the earliest of these pieces, *The Eight Verses of St. Bernard,* was used by King Henry V at Mass in his chapel.[17] The *Devowte Invocacioun to Sainte Denys* was written while Lydgate was in Paris (ca. 1426) for Charles VII of France.[18] Two shorter pieces, the *Prayer of St. Thomas* and *To St. Robert of Bury,* were linked in their origin to the shrines of these saints.[19] Schirmer speculates that the second and more substantial *Prayer to St. Thomas of Canterbury* was also commissioned by the monastery located there.[20] Finally, some of the poems to women saints were connected with Lydgate's powerful women patronesses, for example, the *Invocation to Seynte Anne* written for Countess Anne of Stafford.[21]

The effects Lydgate achieves in these prayers vary from short invocatory pieces to lengthy and intricate devotional lyrics. Among the first group are several miscellaneous pieces designed to introduce longer prayers, like the two-stanza "A Praise of St. Anne," or short prayers written to be worked into the services for the feast-days of the various saints, like the simple, but effective, *A Prayer to Seynt Michaell* and *A Prayer to Gaubriell.* Each of these one-stanza prayers isolate the salient feature of the saint, Michael as the "hevenly championn" and Gabriel as the bringer of tidings to Mary, and ask for the saint's help and protection. More miscellaneous in nature are the prayers *To St. Katherine, St. Margaret, and St. Mary Magdalene, To St. Ositha,* and *To St. Ursula and the Eleven Thousand Virgins.*[22] These short pieces, for the most part, are pedestrian in style and technique and fail to exploit the rich tradition of material available about the saints. The longer *Prayer to St. Leonard* and *Prayers to Ten Saints* are constructed more ambitiously as self-contained poems. The *Prayer to St. Leonard* opens with an invocatory stanza to the saint in a skillfully controlled style, embellished with alliteration:

Reste and reffuge to folk dysconsolat
Fader off pyte and consolacyoun,

> Callid recomfort to folk desolat,
> Souereyn socour in Trybulacioun,
> Vertuous visitour to folkis in prysoun,
> Blissed Leonard! graunte of thy goodnesse,
> To pray Iesu with hooll affeccyoun
> To saue þi servauntis fro myschef & distresse.
> (ll. 1–8)

The next three stanzas celebrate the saint as the patron of the exiled, the poor, the sick, and the oppressed, while the last two stanzas conclude by turning our attention from the world of suffering to the world of eternal gladness in heaven. The *Prayers to Ten Saints* compresses a wealth of material into twelve ballad stanzas, cataloging in the first five stanzas the feats of five heroic male saints—St. Denis, St. George, St. Christopher, St. Blasius, and St. Giles—and in the last five stanzas the experiences of five important women saints—St. Catherine, St. Margaret, St. Martha, St. Christine, and St. Barbara. A two-stanza invocation divides the two sections of the poem. As Schirmer points out, both the arrangement of the material in this poem and the heroic emphasis sets the work off from conventional litany poems.[23] The political undercurrent in Lydgate's references to the first two saints, St. Denis, the patron saint of France, and St. George of England, is also original.

In several of the longer prayers, Lydgate develops more conspicuously the invocatory style he introduces in these lyrics. His effort to create an amplified and elevated medium of praise is especially apparent in four poems, the *Invocation to Seynte Anne,* the *Prayer to St. Edmund, A Prayer to St. Thomas of Canterbury,* and the *Devowte Invocacioun to Sainte Denys.*[24] The *Invocation* is the least elaborate of the four with occasional flourishes of high style, for example, in the verbal display of stanzas 7 and 8, which contain highly wrought images, reduplication of expression, and wordplay. The poems to St. Edmund, St. Thomas, and St. Denis, the patron saints of Bury St. Edmunds, the bishopric of Canterbury, and France, turn the elevated invocatory style to a combined religious and political purpose. In each of these lyrics, Lydgate develops a highly mannered medium, characterized by elaborate wordplay, striking coinages, internal echoing, repetition, and reduplication of expression. The effect ranges from elegant stanzas of praise to overtly artificial lines in which the sense of the passage almost is lost. In its best moments, the high style Lydgate develops in these three poems serves to reinforce the central theme of each of the poems, the saint as the protector of the country or region. Thus, Lydgate introduces Edmund as "Glorious Edmund! kyng of Estyngolond" (l. 1) and, in several skillful stanzas, creates a stately and dignified version of the saint as the champion of the country:

> Geyn Lucyfer, fader of pompe and pride,
>   Pray Crist to sende us dreed with humylyte;
> Geyn fals rancour, envie to sette a syde,
>   That we may leue in parfit charite.
>   Geyn flesshly lustys, clennesse & chastite,
> Through al þi fraunchise lat vertu spryng and spreede,
>   That pees be kept in euery Comounte,
> As ther cheef patroun diffende hem in þer neede.
> (ll. 33–40)

The lines in this stanza are carefully controlled; the verbal repetition, alliteration, and reduplication of expression extend rather than undermine the heroic stature of Edmund as the defender of the people. Likewise, the opening stanza of *A Prayer to St. Thomas of Canterbury* effectively exploits the image of Thomas as the "Synguler shepperde!," the "gardeyn of Christis folde" who protects his "sheep" against enemies. Lydgate's alliteration and wordplay give added emphasis to the conflict between the "shepherd" and the "raueynous wolues" against whose "forward furious violence" he makes resistance.

In contrast to his exploitation of high style in many of the prayers, Lydgate engages in an interesting experimentation with the pathetic style in one prayer, *To St. Robert of Bury.* Inspired by Chaucer in the *Prioress' Tale* and in the Ugolino episode of the *Monk's Tale,* he sentimentalizes Robert's fate as a child martyr, introducing emotionalized outbursts and language that underscores Robert's helplessness and innocence:

> Slayn in childhood by mortal violence,
>   Allas! it was a pitous thing to see
> A sowkyng child, tendre of Innocence,
>   So to be scourged, and naylled to a tre;
>   Thou myghtyst crie, thou spak no woord, parde,
> With-oute language makyng a pitous soun,

Pray for all tho, knelyng on thy kne,
That do reuerence on-to the passioun.
(ll. 9–16)

Lydgate's adaptation of the earlier pathetic style in English to the form of a prayer produces a moving and original tribute to the patron saint of his monastery.

Passion Poems

Although we might expect a development of the emotionalized style of *The Prayer to St. Edmund* in the poems of Christ's passion, Lydgate turns away from this style and the intimate suffering of Christ described in earlier Middle English lyrics to the penitential value of the scenes. He treats Christ's passion not as an opportunity for pathos but as a sacrifice that is a stimulus to repentance. The poems urge man to contemplate the fact of the Crucifixion, to imprint the act in his mind, in order to strengthen his resolve to cleanse himself from sins. Thus, although Lydgate includes descriptions of the agonies of the Cross in these poems, these details are presented without emotive impact. Rather, they are collected as evidence of Christ's strength and resolve. Lydgate's stylistic energy is directed toward elevating Christ's human suffering to bring it out of the realm of man's experience.

The three short lyrics, *The Dolorous Pyte of Crystes Passioun, A Prayer Upon the Cross,* and *Cristes Passioun,* illustrate this emphasis.[25] The first two poems were designed to serve as texts to pictures of the Crucifixion. Both poems are self-consciously executed. In *The Dolorous Pyte,* Lydgate exploits the refrain and the dignified style of many of the stanzas to give the account a heroic quality as he presents Christ on the Cross as man's defense, his "coote armure, brest plate & habirioun" (l. 21) against sin. *A Prayer upon the Cross* is more intricately structured with the five ballad stanzas linked by a refrain and recurrent rhyme scheme of only three rhymes in forty lines. But despite this artistic effort, the description of Christ on the Cross degenerates into a laborious list. *Cristes Passioun,* somewhat longer than the *Dolorous Pyte* and the *Prayer Upon the Cross,* provides Lydgate with a considerable opportunity to amplify and elevate his matter. Characteristically, he expands each detail with energy, but finally the effect is destroyed by his excessive elaboration.

Lydgate's most effective treatment of Christ's passion is found in two long poems, the *Fifteen Ooes of Christ* and the *Seying of the Nightingale.*[26] In the *Fifteen Ooes of Christ,* Lydgate expands the vision of the Passion into an ambitious forty-two-stanza hymn to Christ by adding a *meditatio* and recurrent invocations. The poem opens with an impressive prayer to Christ as man's source of sweetness, joy, and comfort. The memory of his sacrifice, a supreme gesture of love for mankind, provokes a description of the main stages of the Passion. This account is interspersed with several stanzas of "Oracio," which, in the section on the Cross, turn into a lament with alternating hymnic and invocatory stanzas and narrative passages. The result is a heightened version of the events in which the narrative is overlaid with the speaker's response. The various forms of invocation to Christ build as the poem progresses—"O blyssed lord my lord," "O gracyous Iesu!," "Mercyfull Iesu!," "O Iesu! Iesu! callid Alpha and Omega," "O hooly Iesu!" "O sothfast Iesu!," "O myghty Iesu! of Iuda the lyown"—creating an atmosphere of increasing admiration. By the sustained elevation of style in this poem, Lydgate thus attempts to transfer the human sacrifice of Christ from a worldly to a nonworldly plane.

A Seying of the Nightingale is a free rendering of the *Philomela* by the thirteenth-century religious lyricist and Franciscan friar, John Peckham. A famous poem in the Middle Ages, Peckham's Passion lyric represents the song of the nightingale, which lasts from morning until its death in the evening, as an allegory of Christ's Passion, the ages of the world, and the life of man. In Peckham's poem, the nightingale defines by her song the hours of Prime, Tierce, Sexte, and Nones, singing her heart out for love of Christ until she dies at evening. Peckham's form is followed closely by another fifteenth-century poem on the nightingale, once believed to have been written by Lydgate for the duchess of Buckingham.[27] This poem is a compact and carefully constructed piece with a short introduction and a systematic treatment of the allegory. MacCracken first eliminated the poem from the Lydgate canon on the grounds that it differed too much in style and strategy from his other nightingale poem, and most critics have agreed with this determination.[28] In contrast to Peckham's poem and to the other fifteenth-century versions, Lydgate's *Seying of the Nightingale* is discursive and allusive. The poem opens with an elaborate description of the spring evening. All of the birds have finished singing and have retired for the night.

Only the nightingale remains, and the eavesdropping poet listens to her complaint about false lovers. In the body of the poem, the narrator falls asleep and an angelic messenger appears to interpret her song as a memento of Christ's love for mankind and His suffering. This explanation is developed more fully in lines 133–54 by an allusion to Isaiah 63:1 and in lines 155–231 by an account of Christ's words on the Cross and by an amplified catalog of images for the Cross. The final two sections of the poem provide a meditation on Christ's death and His last plea to God, drawing upon the language and imagery of the *Song of Songs* to extend the poem's central theme of divine love. Although Lydgate's version of Peckham's poem is thus massive and digressive, it has an effective underlying design and an appealing mixture of secular poetic elaboration and biblical amplification.

Finally, Lydgate incorporates a version of Christ's Passion in an interesting autobiographical poem, the *Testament*.[29] The poem is divided into four parts with a climatic "Vide" or meditation on the Passion. The first section, a skillful panegyric of Jesus, provides an elaborate interpretation of His name in terms of the rewards of salvation. The second section introduces a retrospective vision of the poet's childhood as a period of dissipation and wildness. Using the spring metaphor as an emblem of the alluring but transitory nature of youth, Lydgate laments his misdeeds and implicitly warns against following his example. The third part, which contains the poet's plea to Jesus to accept his confession, offers a passionate prayer to Jesus as a source of mercy and refuge. The final section, the most intriguing to modern readers, represents the poet's confession proper and is full of lively autobiographical remarks about the sins of Lydgate's youth. Here Lydgate portrays himself as a wanton, profligate, and irresponsible person, bare of "all vertu and pacience" (l. 737) until, at age fifteen, he saw the crucifix with the word "Vide" written upon it. The concluding eighteen stanzas, linked by the recurring command "beholde," join the sections on Jesus and the autobiographical sections in an original way as the poet elaborates upon the message of the word he found on the Cross and directs man's attention to Christ's Passion and crucifixion:

Beholde, o man! lyft vp thyn eye, and see
  What mortall peyne I suffre for thi trespace,
With pietous voys I crye, and sey to the,

> Beholde my woundes, behold my blody face,
> Beholde the rebukes that do me so manace,
> Beholde my enemyes that do me so despice,
> And how that I to reforme the to grace,
> Was like a lambe offred in sacryfice.
> (ll. 754–61)

Thus, although both the testament sections and the descriptions of the Passion have considerable precedents in vernacular literature, Lydgate's clever interweaving of the two traditions is original and effective.

Saints' Lives

Lydgate gives a similar literary emphasis to the majority of his saints' lives. Following in the footsteps of Chaucer, who in the *Second Nun's Tale* turns the direction of the genre in English from its primarily didactic function in church use to the formation of legends of independent artistic merit for a more sophisticated reading public, Lydgate attempts to match and surpass his master in poetic skill. But while Chaucer's conspicuous artistry in the *Second Nun's Tale* brings to the forefront an underlying concern of the saints' life genre itself, the relation of the realm of human activity to a world beyond man's word, sight, and endeavor, Lydgate's literary elaboration serves to overwhelm our senses, to move us to awe and admiration rather than to a consideration of the sentence of his matter. His effort as poet to elevate his material directs our attention to the legends as objects of veneration and renown and represents a new phase in the development of the verse legend.[30]

In some of the shorter legends, including the *Legend of St. George,* written for the brotherhood of London armorers, and the *Legend of St. Petronilla,* written for the lepers' hospital of St. Petronilla at Bury, Lydgate's literary emphasis appears only in an incipient form.[31] The major part of his effort is directed toward the stylistic elevation of the familiar story by means of courtly diction, artistic versification, and aureation to enhance the renown of his hero or heroine. Lydgate's version of the Legend of St. George, for example, is stately, abstract, and decorous compared with the colloquial and explicitly violent account in the *Legenda Aurea.* After a prologue of three Chaucerian stanzas that link George, the protector of England, with the Order of the Garter and interpret the meaning of his name,

Lydgate treats George's life as a model of the chivalrous knight. Omitting the crude details of the battles and torments of the *Legenda,* he describes George with the polish and elegance of the courtly romance.

The legends of St. Margaret, St. Giles, and St. Austin at Compton provide more extended and elaborate efforts to develop a sophisticated literary form of the saints' life.[32] The *Legend of St. Margaret,* written for Lady March, follows the structural design of the *Second Nun's Tale* with a lengthy prologue, an extended interpretation of Margaret's name, a lofty invocation, a central narrative section, and an elaborate envoy. In developing the narrative section, Lydgate omits unessential elements, for example, the realistic detail and descriptions of the tortures found in other versions. Strategically, he strips the scenes of their mundane reference points and removes Margaret's actions from the realm of the human and commonplace reality by his choice of language. The actual plot is subordinated to the verbalization of the characters as Lydgate reorganizes his sources to reduce the number of speakers and expand the speeches and introduce additional monologues. The effect he achieves is a stately and elevated account of Margaret's life in which Christian, courtly, and heroic visions blend. Similarly, in the *Legend of St. Giles* and the *Legend of St. Austin at Compton,* Lydgate sacrifices the narrative element to his overriding artistic concern.[33] In the *Legend of St. Giles,* the story of a hermit who was revered in England and Scotland, he abandons the conventional narrative and casts the work in the form of a direct address to the saint in the second-person singular. The result is a medium between sustained invocation and prayer in which the rhapsodic celebration of the saint is extended for forty-one stanzas which culminate in a formal prayer. Finally, in the *Legend of St. Austin at Compton,* a remonstrance to pay tithes, Lydgate overlays the story with a profusion of ornament, stylistic elaboration, and aureation. Our attention thus often focuses more significantly on style than on story. In a different way in each of these legends, Lydgate deflects his energy away from the development of the narrative itself to the literary potential of the legend.

In contrast to his treatment in these shorter legends, in the two long lives of St. Edmund and St. Alban, Lydgate develops full-fledged epic legends of sustained narrative interest.[34] The *Life of St. Edmund and St. Fremund,* a work of 3,693 lines written at the request of Abbot Curteys for Henry VI after his visit to Bury in 1433–34, relates in three books the life of the martyred king, St. Edmund, the patron of the monastery at Bury, the deeds of his nephew, Fremund, king of Mercia, who avenged Edmund's death, and the miracles associated with these martyrs. The prologue introduces Edmund in terms of the triple crown of the East Angles, of martyrdom, and of chastity, and the heavenly crowns of Henry VI. Book 1 reiterates these themes in a second prologue, provides an elaborate modesty topos, and prayer to the saint as the patron of Bury St. Edmunds, and finally turns to the story of Edmund's rise to the throne. With considerable stylistic elevation, Lydgate recounts Edmund's life and passion as a series of memorable scenes, most notably the passing on of the rule at Offa's death, the coronation itself, and the description of Edmund's arms. The second book deals with the enemies pitched against Edmund who ultimately martyr him. Book 3 turns to the account of Fremund, the son of Offa and Bothild, Edmund's sister, highlighting Fremund's defeat of the Danish enemies before his own martyrdom. In the middle of book 3, Lydgate appends to the account of Fremund a review of the miracles of St. Edmund and concludes with a formal prayer for Henry VI and an envoy. Although the contents of this book are somewhat miscellaneous in nature, the overall effect is sonorous and impressive. The miracles of Edmund serve as a climax to the battles of the two kings, while the concluding prayer reiterates several of Lydgate's favorite themes—the danger of war, the importance of peace and justice, and the appropriate use of royal power in the service of God. Stylistically, the work recalls at times both the epic grandeur of the more effective portions of the *Troy Book* and the intricate working of such elevated political poems as the "Prayer for the King, Queen, and People."

Six years after Lydgate completed the *Life of St. Edmund,* the abbot of St. Albans, Whethamstede, commissioned Lydgate to write a similar double life of St. Alban, the patron saint of his monastery, and St. Amphibalus, who converted Alban to Christianity. For this work, Lydgate earned substantial payment and prestige.[35] The poem, approximately 4,724 lines, represents a culmination of the process of rhetorical embellishment of the saints' life. In narrating the life of St. Alban, Lydgate creates a national Christian epic, massive in its structure and stylistically elaborate. The work, with its excessive amplification, repeated classical and astrological allusions, and aureate language, is even more conspicuously literary than the *Life of*

St. Edmund. Book 1, which opens with the usual modesty topos, describes Amphibalus's conversion at Rome and his training in Christian knighthood with long digressions on chivalry, the ceremony of knighting, the ensuing tournament, and the arms of Alban and Offa. These digressions, together with Lydgate's allegorical and moralistic interpolations and set-speeches, take up more space than the actual narrative and give the poem an expansive and long-winded quality. Book 1 ends with an epic account of the action in Britain as disturbances are put down, Alban is sent to England for the coronation of a new king, and Amphibalus flees the persecution of Christians in Rome. Book 2 narrates the conversion of Alban by Amphibalus with long digressions on the nature of Christianity and the Passion of Alban. These passages, which comprise more than a quarter of the book, culminate in the invocatory tribute to Christ as hero, the model for Alban and Amphibalus. The third and final book, as in the *Life of St. Edmund,* recounts Alban's miracles and the conversion of the people of Wales through Amphibalus' teaching. Although the *Life of St. Alban* finally is more ambitious in its effort to create an epic-legend than the earlier saints' lives, it is less successful than *St. Edmund* because of the mass of irrelevant matter Lydgate introduces which often impedes the progress of the narrative and tries the reader's patience.

Lydgate's tendencies in the saints' lives toward amplification and elevation of style, toward the heroic, and, in the longer lives, toward epic action, had a marked impact on the literary form of the saints' life in the fifteenth century. The important poets who turned to this form—Osborn Bokenham, the author of the *Legends of Hooly Women;* John Capgrave, who wrote a *Legend of St. Catherine,* a *Vitae* of St. Augustine and St. Gilbert; and Henry Bradshaw, who wrote a life of St. Werburge—relied more on Lydgate than on Chaucer for their model. These poets developed the features Lydgate introduces, particularly the blending of the courtly and religious styles, the rhetorical rendering of emotion, and the ambitious attenuation and heroization of the action. In their hands, the characteristics of Lydgate's treatment become stereotyped.

Marian Hymns

The last group of religious poems, the Marian hymns, represent the high point of Lydgate's effort to develop a new medium and form of religious praise. These poems dramatize the shift in emphasis in the religious lyric from the simple, pious fervor of the Franciscan and Bernardine poems, with their intimate and unpretentious style, to a rhetorical and mannered celebratory style. Lydgate's poems do not seek to bridge the gap between God and man by presenting God and Mary in human form or to establish an intimate love relation between man and God by means of the courtly mode, but rather to reassert the sacred character of the deity by moving man to awe and admiration. Mary thus no longer finds form in these poems as the consoling lover or the mother ministering to her child, but as the majestic queen of heaven. The style Lydgate develops—with its elaborate vocabulary, aureation, and alliteration, its mystical ornamentation, its excessive imagery, allusions, and invocations—overwhelms the reader and establishes Mary as an object of veneration.

The concern of Lydgate's Marian hymns with invoking our admiration for Mary's glory is apparent when one compares his lyrics with Chaucer's "ABC," the most famous earlier example of a Marian celebration in English. The difference between this poem and Lydgate's "Ballade at the Reverence of Our Lady" and "To Mary, the Queen of Heaven," is not simply one of increased aureation and rhetorical elaboration but involves a changed conception of the role of style and the purpose of the lyric itself.[36] Chaucer opens with a stately and dignified address to the Virgin and the poem reaches a few moments of high style in Lydgate's sense, for example in stanza 14:

> O verrey light of eyen that ben blynde,
> O verrey lust of labour and distresse,
> O tresoreere of bountee to mankynde,
> Thee whom God ches to mooder for humblesse!
> (ll. 105–8)

But this is not Chaucer's main purpose in the lyric. Rather, he subordinates style to his theme of Mary as man's refuge, his comfort. Lydgate focuses all of his effort on his medium; the elaboration of Mary's praise in his hymn becomes an act of devotion. The style Lydgate develops forms an essential part of the poem's meaning as his words create an artifact, a tribute to Mary's glory.

After the "Ballade at the Reverence of Our Lady," the best example of Lydgate's technique in the Marian poems is provided by two lyrics, "To Mary, the Queen of Heaven" and "Ave Jesse Virgula."[37] In these poems, Lydgate adds little that is new to the content of the lyric. His language and images are drawn from traditional sources—the Old Testament text and commentaries, particularly the *Song of Solomon* and *Ecclesiasticus,* and the Latin hymnic tradition. The construction of the poems, like the progress of a litany, is an arbitrary succession with each segment joined by the speaker's rapt invocatory tone. The meaning of individual lines, which depends on erudite allusions and intellectual associations, is often difficult, and the reader is forced to decipher the startling images.

In "To Mary, the Queen of Hevene," based on the antiphon *Ave Regina Celorum,* Lydgate bombards us with a dazzling array of epithets for the Virgin. Carefully orchestrating the poem, he groups the most striking associations to form stanza-long invocations:

> Celestial cipresse set vpon Syon,
> Hiest Cidre of perfit holynesse,
> Carboncle of charite and grene emerawd ston,
> Hool & vnbroken by virgynal clennesse,
> O Saphir loup al swellyng to represse,
> Off cankred sores & venymous feloun,
> In gostly woundes be ther gouerneresse
> To thy .v. Ioies þat haue deuocioun.
> (ll. 9–16)

The language is heavily latinate and often ingenious in its erudition and wordplay. In the envoy, the elaborately crafted imagery of Mary, Queen of Heaven, is finally offered as a memento of her five joys.

In "Ave Jesse Virgula," a paraphrase of a Marian hymn now lost, Lydgate combines the invocatory form with an even more breathtaking array of images, epithets, and allusions than we find in the other lyrics. In many of the stanzas, he extends the invocations to such a degree that the immediate sense of his lines is obscured:

> Haile, holsom cypres, growyng in Syon!
> Haile, fons signatus, most clere cristallyne!
> Haile, gold in Trone of prudent Salamon
> Gostly closed, most hevenly in devyne!
> Haile, to-fore whose brest all grace dide shyne,
> From phebus paleys, bilded supra sidera;

Haile, hevenly gardyn, welle in divyne,
Haile, flos campi, o Ave Iesse virgula!
(ll. 9–16)

The poem is a veritable catalog of Marian imagery. In turn, Lydgate includes all of the traditional categories—Mary as the tabernacle, the window of heaven, the star of the sea, the rose, the laurel, the myrrh, the day-star, the lantern and light, the most precious of stones, the product of the three theological and the four cardinal virtues. After elaborating each image, Lydgate concludes the catalog with the most spectacular examples—*Eva* transformed into *Ave* and the vision of the Apostle John with Mary clothed in a sun with twelve stars and precious stones voiding the darkness, a moon under her feet in token of God's victory over vices and His mercy for sinners. Finally, Lydgate sums up Mary's power in a triple anagram on her name. In addition to his manipulation of imagery, in this poem Lydgate attempts to extend his language by introducing in each stanza a Latin half line, linked by rhyme with the refrain to create a rich internal echoing of image and meaning. As in "Te Deum Laudamus," he frequently combines Latin, latinate, and aureate English in such a manner that the bounds between each language are obliterated.

In addition to the antiphonal hymns and the invocatory poems, Lydgate develops a third category of Marian poems, the celebration of the Joys of the Virgin. The number of joys varies in the poems. Originally five, the figure later expanded to fifteen, a number that became common in England. Lydgate focuses on the five joys in "To Mary Queen of Heaven," "To Mary Star of Jacob," and "Gaude virgo mater Christi."[38] The "Ave Maria" expands the joys to seven, linking the treatment of the seven joys with a Latin refrain from the salutation "Ave Maria gracis plena." The two poems, "The Fyftene Ioyes of Oure Lady" and "The Fifteen Joys and Sorrows of Mary," finally develop this theme in its most attenuated form. In these poems, Lydgate not only expands his matter to form a litanylike prayer of salutation, but he also elevates his imagery considerably by changing familiar images like the morning dew to gold and silver. The *gaudia,* in Lydgate's treatment, become extended invocations that move the reader to awe and admiration of Mary as the "Emp[e]resse in heuene glorified."

It is in turning from the Marian hymns to Lydgate's more extended treatment of Mary in the *Life of Our Lady,* however, that we find the most significant example of his experimentation with sacred form.[39] The poem is a large, open-ended form, more of an extended celebration than a life. In it, Lydgate virtually abandons the continuous narrative to create a unique form and medium that accentuates the nobility of his subject. Though unfinished, the *Life of Our Lady* is perhaps Lydgate's most impressive piece of religious writing. Book 1 provides a good example of Lydgate's technique in this poem. In the prologue to this book, Lydgate introduces his theme and raises the artistic problems he will confront in this work, exploiting with striking originality the traditional image of Mary as the star to suggest both of these concerns. The section opens with the narrator's address to his "thoughtful herte, plunged in distresse" in need of renewal both spiritually and artistically. In this state, the narrator bids his heart awaken and look at the light of the star that gladdens our hemisphere. The next six stanzas define Mary's powers to renew man in terms of highly successful variations on this image as the North Star, the haven from death's brink, the star which never declines, the star that dries the bitter tears of Aurora, and the star that bore the bright "sonne" with light of grace, to "voiden all our tene." With a last transformation of the image, Lydgate suggests the need for Mary's aid not only to alleviate the "tene" of the human condition, but also to enable him to execute his craft as a poet and write her praise.

The body of book 1 narrates Mary's birth, her youthful beauty, the selection of her husband, and her marriage. But the actual events in Lydgate's treatment are much less important than his exploitation of the narrative as an opportunity for a prolonged celebration of Mary. Lydgate opens with a magnificent passage to describe Mary's birth. In contrast to some of his short lyrics, the images here are perfectly controlled and move gracefully from the familiar to the more striking or unusual associations. Beginning with the conventional image of the garden, he likens Mary's birth to the blooming of a "flour of vertue" (l. 64) which had been enclosed for many springs "with holsome leves swote" (l. 65), and, finally by grace sprang from the root of God. He turns from the virtues of this flower—its preserving and healing ability, its color, its sweetness—to a celebration of Nazareth, the city that contained this garden, a city more royal than Troy, Rome, or a catalog of famous cities, to a comparison of Mary with the other worthy heroes who inhabited these cities, to the prophecies about the miraculous nature of this flower, to the greatest miracle of all, the flower as the resting place for the Holy Ghost, the flower that symbolically combines the white of the lily, the red of the rose, and the purple of the violet.

Lydgate dramatically describes the actual birth of Mary by means of two striking biblical and literary parallels—Jacob wrestling with the angel and the miraculous birth of Minerva from "the fadirs sapience" (l. 178). In this section, he introduces miracle after miracle to emphasize the wondrous nature of Mary's youth. The section culminates with a thirty-eight-stanza celebration of her unsurpassing beauty and her holy nature in which Lydgate amplifies and elevates his description by citing the earlier attempts of Solomon, Anselm, and the writer of the Book of Elizabeth to define Mary's uniqueness. Each of these passages, in turn, elaborates one aspect of Mary's renown, the first her fairness and perfection as the chosen one of the Holy Ghost, the second Mary as the embodiment of the seven gifts of the Holy Ghost, and the last as the perfect servant of God. The celebration ends with Mary's thirteen-stanza prayer to God. Again we pause for a brief narrative section—the attempt of Abiathar to wed Mary to his son, the selection of a husband for Mary, the miraculous appearance of the dove on Joseph's rod, their chaste marriage, and Mary's continued service to God. The narrative stanzas are climaxed by a splendid celebration of Mary's perfection and Lydgate's lament that he cannot do justice to his sacred subject within the limitations of the language.

Book 1 is typical of Lydgate's strategy throughout the poem, to create increasingly strong waves of celebration, brief passages of narrative which culminate in extended praise of Mary. The effect is that of a prolonged Marian hymn rather than a continuous narrative. The poem not only contains some of the finest passages of Lydgate's verse, for example, the description of the virgin birth and Lydgate's inspired defense of its miraculous nature in book 2 and the elaborate praise of Mary as the mother of Christ with which book 3 closes, but also is one of the high points of English religious poetry.

Underlying the various kinds of religious poems to which Lydgate turns is an awareness of the dilemma of the human poet who must create a medium worthy of sacred objects in the vernacular. Repeatedly seeking to "redresse" or reform his style, Lydgate attempts to develop a new mode of religious praise in English that moves the reader to an appreciation of the significance of the poet's matter. This concern becomes a major theme in many of the poems and distinguishes Lydgate's instructional and devotional lyrics from earlier English examples. The style Lydgate introduces is marked by elaborate alliteration, aureation, verbal echoing, and an accumulation of epithets, images, and allusions. In most cases, the treatment is conspicuously literary and directs our attention toward the poems as artistic production or artifacts rather than toward the emotive or devotional value of the matter. Although Lydgate's success in these poems is uneven, his experimentation influenced the practices of many fifteenth-century poets.

Chapter Eight
Lydgate's Achievement and Impact

Although Lydgate was admired by his contemporaries and successors for three centuries, he is today a considerably underrated poet. Condemned by Ritson in 1802 as a "voluminous, prosaick, and driveling monk," a "stupid and disgusting author," Lydgate has suffered both from the legacy of these remarks and from the recurrent comparison with his master, Chaucer.[1] But despite the negative view that has passed from critic to critic in the last 150 years, the fact remains that Lydgate was a major force in fifteenth-century literature. Ranked by his peers the equal of Chaucer and Gower,[2] he stands out not only by the sheer volume of his writing but also by the variety and scope of his poetry, the range of his experimentation, and the widespread support of numerous important patrons. In the more than 145,000 lines of his verse, Lydgate tries his hand at all of the poetic forms that come to dominate the fifteenth century, often leaving these forms permanently and significantly changed. His position in the period and the discrepancy between the medieval and Renaissance and the modern assessments of his accomplishments make it important to reappraise the significance of his work.

The fifteenth- and early sixteenth-century responses to Lydgate provide considerable insight into the reasons his contemporaries valued his writing. The majority of writers isolate two aspects of Lydgate's work for particular praise—its rhetorical nature and its sententiousness. Linking Lydgate with Chaucer and Gower as the three poets who made English literature worthy of admiration, they commend his effort to elevate and extend his native tongue. As early as ca. 1450, the author of an *Account of Lydgate* praises him as "a great ornament of ye English Toung" while Ashby, in the prologue to the *Active Policy of a Prince* (ca. 1470), refers to "Maisters Gower, Chaucer & Lydgate" as the first poets of the nation who produced a significant literary language:

Embelysshing oure englisshe tendure algate
  Firste finders to oure consolacion
Off fresshe, douce englisshe and formacion
  Of newe balades, not vsed before
  By whome we all may haue lernyng and lore.[3]

This praise is confirmed by Bokenham, Metham, Bradshaw, Hawes, Caxton, Rastell, and the Scots poets, Douglas, Dunbar, and Lindsay.[4] Metham's version (1448–49) is particularly interesting in its explicit definition of the stylistic features that distinguish Lydgate's writing—his rhetorical terms, his aureate language, and his skillful images:

Eke Ion Lydgate, sumtyme monke off Byry,
Hys bokys endytyd with termys off retoryk
And halff chongyd Latyne, with conseytys off poetry
And craffty imagynacionys off thingys fantastyk. . . .[5]

To the recurrent praise of Lydgate's rhetorical style, many writers add an appreciation of the fruitful nature of his work. Feylde and Hawes at the beginning of the sixteenth century, for example, both rank Lydgate higher than Chaucer and Gower for these qualities. Feylde, in the prologue to the "Contrauerse bytwene a Louer and a Jaye," compares the three poets:

Chaucer floure of rethoryke eloquence
Compyled bokes pleasaunt and meruayllous
After hym noble Gower experte in scyence
Wrote moralytyes herde and delycyous
But Lydgate's workes are fruytefull and sentencyous
Who of his bokes hathe redde the fyne
He wyll hym call a famus rethorycyne.[6]

In the *Pastime of Pleasure,* Hawes reveals a similar preference, devoting only two lines to Gower, nineteen to Chaucer, and sixty-three to Lydgate, "the moste dulcet sprynge / Of famous rethoryke." Summing up his achievement in an impassioned eulogy, he compares Lydgate to the "vayne" poets who "fayne no fables" but compose only ballads and trifles.[7] Similarly, in the prologue to the *Pastime,* Hawes singles Lydgate out for his ability to present truth "vnder a colour" like the poets of old.[8]

The fifteenth- and sixteenth-century poets' praise of Lydgate corresponds significantly to Lydgate's assessment of Chaucer as the "flower of Poets in our English tung."[9] In his numerous eulogies of Chaucer, Lydgate emphasizes the earlier poet's role in establishing English as a serious literary language. Chaucer "enlumined our language with flowers of rethorick eloquence." He "made firste to distille and reyne / The golde dewe droppis of speche and eloquence / In-to oure tounge" and illuminated our "rude speche."[10] Before Chaucer, English was crude, boistrous, and of little reputation. Finally, Lydgate emphasizes the connection between Chaucer's rhetoric and the significance of his text, praising his ability to keep "in substaunce / / The sentence hool / withoute variance, / / Voyding the Chaf / sothly for to seyn, / / Enlumynyng / þe trewe piked greyn."[11] In placing English on the map of serious literature, Lydgate asserts, Chaucer belongs to the tradition of great national poets: "Daunt In Itaille, Virgile in Rome town, / Petrak in Florence hadde al hys plesaunce, / And prudent Chaucer in Brutis Albioun."[12]

Lydgate's contemporaries and immediate successors, in turn, honor him by representing his achievement as a continuation of the tradition of important vernacular poets. The author of *A Rebuke to Lydgate* (ca. 1440) first makes explicit the transference of the role of leader of the English poets from Chaucer to Lydgate. Since Chaucer is "dede and buryde in thy graue . . . to the monke of bury now speke I / For thy connyng ys syche and eke thy grace / After chaucer to occupye his place."[13] Likewise, in the *Pastime of Pleasure,* Hawes directs our attention from Gower to Chaucer to Lydgate, indicating the preemince of Lydgate as "maister" by devoting only two lines to Gower, nineteen to Chaucer, and sixty-three lines of elaborate praise to Lydgate.[14] Shortly afterward, Dunbar, Rastell, Lindsay, and Skelton all link Lydgate with Gower and Chaucer to form a triumvirate of English poets distinguished for their role in improving and elevating "our vulgar toung" and making English the equivalent of the other significant literary vernaculars.[15] Finally, Copland extends the line of succession of noble English poets from Chaucer to Lydgate to Hawes.[16]

But although Lydgate is linked with Chaucer and Gower as the "primier poetes of this nacion," the ornamentors of the English tongue, he finally moves in a direction as poet that is different from theirs. In his effort to enhance his medium and expand the limits of his forms, Lydgate broadens the base of poetry in English. Turning his pen to subjects previously outside the domain of literature, he acts principally as a craftsman or "rethor" who illuminates and adorns his matter. His stance is that of a public poet whose craft may be summoned by his various patrons to transform occasional events into works of a more permanent nature. As an occasional poet, Lydgate produces both works of considerable merit, in which he manages to create legitimate literary forms out of the demands of the moment, and poems of more mediocre quality.

Behind the diversity of his works, both secular and religious, is a vision of the poet that differs in several ways from the conceptions of most earlier English poets. In Lydgate's view, the poet is an "enluminer" and an orderer who turns his craft to the task of ennobling and civilizing men. Like the mythological figure of Amphion, the poet-king who founded Thebes by the power of his "song," Lydgate envisions his role as one of leading men to order and harmony in the world. The focus of the poet's attention shifts from the heuristic search for Truth and the journey to salvation to the acquisition of wisdom, virtue, and political stability in the world. The poet's eloquence serves to illuminate these concerns and to move men to peace and harmony. The antidote to the destructive power of Fortune, the poet's activity reinforces the values and ideals that ennoble men. Thus, as Lydgate emphasizes in the *Fall of Princes,* the poet not only has the power to write but he also has a sacred obligation to exercise his craft.

Finally, then, one may agree with Skelton, who deviates from the almost unanimous contemporary praise of Lydgate by noting two of his faults—his verbosity and his overly elevated style. As he suggests in "Philip Sparrow," sometimes "It is dyffuse to fynde / The sentence of his mynde."[17] Similarly, in the "Garlande of Laurell," Skelton makes Lydgate address him in a clever parody of his conspicuously crafted style.[18] Despite this criticism, Skelton acknowledges the influence and importance of Lydgate's writing, adding to the reviews of Gower and Chaucer as poets in "Philip Sparrow" that Lydgate "Wryteth after an hyer rate" and "Yet wryteth he in his hynd, / No man that can amend / Those maters that he hath pende."[19] With both Lydgate's deficiencies and his innovations in mind, one must appreciate his position as a poet who sought to expand the province of English literature in directions that became increasingly significant in the fifteenth century.

Notes and References

Preface

1. See, for example, John Metham, *Political, Religious, and Love Poems,* ed. F. J. Furnivall (London, 1866), 307; Thomas Feylde, "Here Begynneth a Lytel Treatyse Called the Contrauerse Bytwene a Louer and a Jaye Lately Complyed," in *Five Hundred Years of Chaucer Criticism and Allusion,* ed. Caroline Spurgeon (1925; reprint, New York, 1960), 1:70; Stephen Hawes, *Pastime of Pleasure,* ed. William E. Mead, EETS, ES, 173 (London, 1928), ll. 1372–1407; William Dunbar, *The Poems of William Dunbar,* ed. William Mackay MacKenzie (1932; reprint, London, 1960), no. 56, ll. 262–70.

2. George Saintsbury, "The English Chaucerians," in *Cambridge History of English Literature,* ed. A. W. Ward and A. R. Waller (1908; reprint, Cambridge, 1963), 2:200.

3. Walter F. Schirmer, *John Lydgate: A Study in the Culture of the XVth Century,* trans. Ann E. Keep (Berkeley and Los Angeles, 1961), xiii. See also "The Importance of the Fifteenth Century to the Study of the English Renaissance," in *English Studies Today,* ser. 1, ed. C. L. Wrenn and G. Bullough (London, 1951), 104–10.

4. Alain Renoir, *The Poetry of John Lydgate* (Cambridge, Mass., 1967), 143.

5. H. S. Bennett, *Chaucer and the Fifteenth Century* (Oxford, 1947); Eleanor P. Hammond, *English Verse Between Chaucer and Surrey* (1927; reprint, New York, 1969), 3–37; Derek Pearsall, *John Lydgate* (London, 1970).

Chapter One

1. *The Minor Poems of John Lydgate,* part 1, ed. Henry Noble MacCracken, EETS, ES, 107 (London, 1911), no. 68, ll. 614–17.

2. See the life records printed in *Temple of Glas,* ed. J. Schick, EETS, ES, 60 (London, 1891), lxxvi. For other collections of Lydgate records, see Schirmer, *John Lydgate,* 21, 246–47; *Secrees of Old Philisoffres,* ed. R. Steele, EETS, ES, 66 (London, 1894), xxiii–xxx; A. B. Emden, *A Biographical Register of the University of Oxford,* 3 vols. (Oxford, 1957–59), 2:1185–86.

3. The first two references are from the register of William Cratfield, abbot of Bury (1389–1414), MS Cotton Tiberius B. ix. fols. 35b, 69b, 85b; Fordham's Register, fols. 234, 238 (Emden, *Biographical Register,*

2:1186). According to a manuscript note in Tyrwhitt's copy of Wayland's *Fall of Princes* (B.L. 838, m. 17), Lydgate was ordained priest by John Fordham, bishop of Ely on Saturday, 7 April 1397.

4. *Anglo-Norman Letters and Petitions from All Souls MS 182,* ed. M. Dominica Legge (Oxford, 1941), pp. 411–12.

5. Ashmole 59, fol. 246; see *The Minor Poems of John Lydgate,* ed. Henry Noble MacCracken, pt. 2, EETS, OS, 192 (London, 1934), 598.

6. *Proceedings of the Privy Council,* ed. H. Nicholas 3:41.

7. *Pilgrimage of the Life of Man,* ed. F. J. Furnivall and Katherine B. Locock, EETS, ES, 77, 83, 92 (London, 1899–1904).

8. See the *dimissio* from the *registrum* of William Curteys reprinted in Schirmer, *John Lydgate,* 91.

9. Steele, *Secrees,* xxiii; Schick, *Temple of Glas,* cxii.

10. *The Poems of William Dunbar,* ed. MacKenzie no. 7, ll. 50–52.

11. Stephen Hawes, *The Conforte of Louers,* in *Stephen Hawes: The Minor Poems,* ed. Florence W. Gluck and Alice Morgan, EETS, ES, 217 (London, 1974), l. 25.

12. John Skelton, "The Garlande of Laurell," in *The Poetical Works of John Skelton,* ed. Alexander Dyce (London, 1843), 1:377, ll. 387–91.

13. A. B. Whittingham, *Bury St. Edmunds Abbey* (London, 1971), 4. For records of the abbey and its history, see *Victoria County History of Suffolk,* ed. W. Page (London, 1907), 2:56–72; Dugdale, *Monastican,* 3:98–176; M. R. James, *On the Abbey of St. Edmunds at Bury,* Cambridge Antiquarian Society, no. 28, 1895; *Memorials of St. Edmunds Abbey,* ed. T. Arnold, Rolls Series, no. 96 (London, 1890–96).

14. Whittingham, *Bury St. Edmunds Abbey,* 4.

15. Ibid., 4–5.

16. *The Chronicle of Jocelin of Brakelond,* trans. H. E. Butler (1949; reprint, London, 1951), 23 ff.

17. Ibid., 72.

18. Ibid.

19. Ibid., 54–55.

20. Schirmer, *John Lydgate,* 15–16; Pearsall, *John Lydgate,* 24.

21. Schirmer, *John Lydgate,* 15–17.

22. *Victoria County History of Suffolk,* 2:96; D. Knowles and R. N. Hadock, *Medieval Religious Houses in England and Wales* (London, 1953), 61.

23. Dugdale, *Monastican,* 3:113 (translated from the *Register Curteys,* fol. 110).

24. *St. Edmund and Fremund,* ed. C. Horstmann, in *Altenglische Legenden* (Heilbronn, 1881), 1:190.

25. *Victoria County History of Suffolk,* 2:65.

26. Ibid., 2:71.

27. M. R. James, "Bury St. Edmunds Manuscripts," *EHR* 41 (1926):251–60.

28. Richard Pynson, ed., *Testament,* reproduced in *Minor Poems,* ed. MacCracken.

29. Shirley MS Add. 16165; Schick, *Temple of Glas,* xxiii.

30. Henry Noble MacCracken, "Additional Light on the *Temple of Glas,*" *PMLA* 23 (1908):128–40; Schirmer, *John Lydgate,* 37–38.

31. Schirmer, *John Lydgate,* 41.

32. Cotton Aug. MS. A IV; Bodl. Digby MS 232 (Bodleian, Oxford); Crawford-Rylands MS (Manchester); Trin. Coll. MS. 0. 5. 2 (Cambridge); Rawl. C. 446 (Bodleian, Oxford).

33. *Troy Book,* ed. Henry Bergen, EETS, ES, 97, 103, 106, 126 (London, 1906–20), 5:3366 ff; hereafter *Troy Book* is cited as *TB* in the text.

34. *Pilgrimage of the Life of Man,* prologue; *Minor Poems,* ed. MacCracken, pt. 1, no. 17.

35. *Minor Poems,* ed. MacCracken, pt. 1, no. 26. For a discussion of Humphrey's role as patron, see K. H. Vickers, *Humphrey Duke of Gloucester* (London, 1907), chaps. 9–10; R. Weiss, *Humanism in England during the 15th Century* (Oxford, 1957), 39 ff; Schirmer, *John Lydgate,* 19–50; Pearsall, *John Lydgate,* 223–30.

36. Eleanor P. Hammond, "Lydgate and Coluccio Salutari," *MP* 25 (1927), 49–57 and "Poet and Patron in the Fall of Princes," *Anglia* 38 (1914):121–36.

37. *Minor Poems,* ed. MacCracken, pt. 2, no. 52.

38. For a useful summary of these accounts, see E. F. Jacob, *The Fifteenth Century 1399–1485,* Oxford History of England, vol. 6 (Oxford, 1961), 1–10.

39. Adam of Usk, *Chronicon Ade de Usk,* ed. E. Maunde Thompson (London, 1876), 27–30.

40. See "Record and Process of the Renunciation of King Richard the Second after the Conquest, and the Acceptance of the same Renunciation together with the deposition of the same king," in *Rot. Parl.* 3:416 f.

41. *Chronique de la traison et mort de Richard II,* English Historical Society Pub., 1846, pp. 106 ff.; M. V. Clarke and V. H. Galbraith, "The Deposition of Richard II," *Bull. John Rylands Lib* 14 (1930):146.

42. *Gesti Henrici Quinti,* trans. F. Taylor and S. Raskell (Oxford, 1975); *Foedora,* 4.2.107.

43. Schirmer, *John Lydgate,* 53.

44. Hoccleve, *Regement of Princes,* in *Hoccleve's Works,* ed. F. J. Furnivall, EETS, ES, 72 (London, 1897), ll. 5377 ff.

45. Jacobs, *The Fifteenth Century,* 193–94.

46. For a useful review of these accounts, see ibid., 201–2.

47. For a description of these favorable accounts, see Schirmer, *John Lydgate,* 53–54.

48. *Siege of Thebes,* ed. A. Erdman and E. Ekwall, EETS, ES, 108, 125 (London, 1911–20), ll. 4645 ff; hereafter cited in the text as *ST.*

49. Ibid., ll. 4645–53: "Item, ut Concordia, Pax et Tranquillitas inter praedicta Franciae et Angliae Regna perpetuo futuris temporibus observentur . . ." (quoted by Pearsall, *John Lydgate,* 156).

50. Schirmer, *John Lydgate,* 82.

51. *Minor Poems,* ed. MacCracken, pt. 2, no. 64.

52. See, for example, *Siege of Thebes,* ll. 183–327; *Fall of Princes,* ed. Henry Bergen, EETS, ES, 121–24 (London, 1924–27), 6:337–43; *Temple of Glas,* l. 1310.

53. *Siege of Thebes,* ll. 184–327.

54. Ibid., ll. 272–74.

55. *Fall of Princes,* 6:337–50, 3487–3500; hereafter cited in the text as *FP.*

56. For a more detailed description of Lydgate's critical terminology, see Lois A. Ebin, "Lydgate's Views on Poetry," *Annuale Mediaevale* 18 (1977):76–105.

Chapter Two

1. *Minor Poems,* ed. MacCracken, pt. 2, nos. 20, 23.

2. For a discussion of the date of these poems, see: J. Schick, *Temple of Glas,* lxxxvii–cxiii; Schirmer, *John Lydgate,* 31–41.

3. *Minor Poems,* ed. MacCracken, pt. 2, nos. 1–8; *Temple of Glas,* ed. John Norton-Smith, in *John Lydgate: Poems* (Oxford, 1966), 67–112; *Resoun and Sensuallyte,* vol. 1, ed. Ernst Sieper, EETS, ES, 84 (1965; reprint, London, 1901).

4. *John Lydgate: Poems,* ed. Norton-Smith, 47–66.

5. Ibid., 160–61.

6. *Minor Poems,* ed. MacCracken, pt. 2, nos. 6–7.

7. Ibid., 379.

8. John Norton-Smith, "Lydgate's Metaphors," *English Studies* 42 (1961):90–93; Alain Renoir, "The Binding Knot: Three Uses of One Image in Lydgate's Poetry," *Neophilologus* 41 (1957):202–4.

9. For a discussion of the manuscripts of the *Temple of Glas,* see Schick, *Temple of Glas,* xvii–xlix.

10. See, for example, ibid., 72; *John Lydgate: Poems,* ed. Norton-Smith, 181.

11. For a discussion of Lydgate's use of images, see Norton-Smith, "Lydgate's Metaphors," 90–93.

12. John Norton-Smith, "Lydgate's Changes in the *Temple of Glas,*" *Medium Aevum* 27 (1958):166–72.

13. Ibid., 167–68.

14. Ibid., 170.

15. This motto was used in England by the Pastons in the fifteenth century. MacCracken suggests, on the basis of Lydgate's changes, that the poem was written for the marriage of William Paston to Agnes Berry in 1420; see *PMLA* 23 (1908):128–40. For an interesting consideration of the question of patronage in the *Temple of Glas,* see J. Wilson, "Poet and Patron in Early Fifteenth Century England: John Lydgate's *Temple of Glas,*" *Parergon* 11 (1975):25–32.

16. See, for example, Pearsall, *John Lydgate,* 107; *John Lydgate's Poems,* ed. Norton-Smith, 178.

17. Schick, *Temple of Glas,* cxxi; Sieper, *Resoun and Sensuallyte,* vol. 2, EETS, ES, 89 (1903; reprint, Oxvford, 1965), 5.

Chapter Three

1. The two stories, for example, appear together in the following English manuscripts: Trinity 0. 5. 2, Royal 18. D. ii, and Digby 230.

2. *Troy Book,* prologue, ll. 75–83.

3. Geoffrey of Monmouth, *Historia regum Britanniae,* ed. J. Hammer, Medieval Academy of America Publications, no. 57 (Cambridge, Mass., 1951).

4. *Sir Gawain and the Green Knight,* ed. J. R. R. Tolkein and E. V. Gordon (1925; reprint, Oxford, 1963), ll. 11–15.

5. Guido delle Colonne, *Historia Destructionis Troiae,* ed. Nathaniel Griffin, Medieval Academy of America Publications, no. 26 (1936; reprint, New York, 1970); trans. Mary Elizabeth Meek (Bloomington, 1974), prologue, ll. 21–32.

6. The Latin text of Dictys is edited by Ferdinand Meister (Leipzig, 1873). For a useful translation and introduction, see *The Trojan War: The Chronicles of Dictys of Crete and Dares the Phrygian,* trans. R. M. Frazer, Jr. (Bloomington, 1966).

7. For the Latin text of Dares, see Werner Eisenhut's edition (Leipzig, 1958).

8. Benoit de St. Maure, *Roman de Troie,* ed. Leopold Constans, Societé des anciens texte français, 6 vols. (Paris, 1904–12).

9. Guido, *Historia.* For a useful analysis of Guido's text as history, see C. David Benson, *The History of Troy in Middle English Literature* (Woodbridge, Suffolk, 1980), 3–31. For a discussion of the relation of Guido, Benoit, Dares, and Dictys, see Nathaniel Griffin, "Un-Homeric Elements in the Medieval Story of Troy," *JEGP* 7 (1907–8):36–38.

10. Morton Bloomfield, "Chaucer's Sense of History," *JEGP* 51 (1952):301–13; reprinted in *Essays and Explorations* (Cambridge, Mass., 1970), 13–26.

11. *Troy Book,* 2.1–76, 1797–1902, 2183–2304, 6640–61, 7836–75; 4:2401–18.

12. Guido, *Historia,* 21:162–77.

13. Guido, *Historia,* 6:185–253; *Troy Book,* 2:2370–2792.

14. See, for example, Pearsall, *John Lydgate,* 122–59. For other useful critical commentaries on Lydgate's *Troy Book,* see Renoir, *The Poetry of John Lydgate,* 52 ff; Schirmer, *John Lydgate,* 42–51; Paul Strohm, "*Storie, Spelle, Geste, Romaunce, Tragedie:* Generic Distinctions in the Middle English Troy Narratives," *Speculum* 46 (1971):351–52.

15. *Troy Book,* 1. 1197–1309; Guido, *Historia,* 2. 116–42.

16. Guido, *Historia,* 2:128–42.

17. *Troy Book,* 1. 1568 ff., 1608 ff., 2098 ff., 2152 ff., 2738 ff., 2863 ff., 3599 ff.

18. For an account of the transmission of these passages, see Gretchen Mieszkowski, *The Reputation of Criseyde 1155–1500, Transactions of the Connecticut Academy of Arts and Sciences* 43 (1971):116–26.

19. *Troy Book,* 4. 1701–1896; Guido, *Historia,* 15. 169–217.

20. Guido, *Historia,* 30:215–30; *Troy Book,* 4.6476–86.

21. *Troy Book,* 4.5209 ff., 5833 ff., 6039 ff., 6441 ff.

22. Pearsall (*John Lydgate,* 151–54) is one of the few critics to note this difference. Compare his description, for example, with Alain Renoir's (*The Poetry of John Lydgate,* 110 ff.). See *Siege of Thebes.* For a brief discussion of the relation of the *Siege of Thebes* to its sources, see Renoir, "The Immediate Source of Lydgate's *Siege of Thebes,*" *SN* 33 (1961):86–95.

23. *Siege of Thebes,* ll. 823 ff., 991 ff., 1476 ff., 1564 ff., 1663 ff., 2664 ff., 3404 ff., 4565.

24. Giovanni Boccaccio, *Genealogia deorum gentilium libri* (Bari, 1951).

25. *Siege of Thebes,* ll. 1236–1649.

26. Ibid., ll. 2998–3504.

27. Ibid., ll. 1874–2122.

28. Ibid., ll. 2794–2988.

29. Ibid., ll. 3726–3821.

30. Quoted by Pearsall, *John Lydgate,* 156.

31. R. W. Ayers, "Medieval History, Moral Purpose, and the Structure of Lydgate's *Siege of Thebes,*" *PMLA* 73 (1958):463–74.

32. For a more detailed discussion of this issue, see my article, "Chaucer, Lydgate, and the 'Myrie Tale,' " *Chaucer Review* 13 (1979):316–36.

33. Geoffrey Chaucer, *The Canterbury Tales,* in *The Works of Geoffrey Chaucer,* ed. F. N. Robinson, 2d ed. (Boston, 1957), IV, E, 9–15.

Chapter Four

1. Aristotle, *Poetics,* ed. Friedrich Solmsen (New York, 1954), chap. 6, ll. 28–29.

2. See, for example, Einhard, *Vita Karoli Magni,* ed. and trans. Evelyn Scherabon (Coral Gables, Fla., 1972); *Chronicles of the Crusades, being Contemporary Narratives of the Crusade of Richard Coeur de Lion by Richard of Devizes and of the Crusade of St. Louis by Lord John de Joinville* (1848; reprint, New York, 1969).

3. Ordericus Vitalis, *Historia ecclesiastica,* ed. A. Le Provost, 5 vols. (Paris, 1838–55); Henry of Huntington, *Historia Anglorum,* ed. Thomas Arnold (London, 1879); William of Malmesbury, *Gesta Regum Anglorum,* ed. William Stubbs, 2 vols. (London, 1887–89).

4. Giovanni Boccaccio, *De casibus illustrium virorum,* ed. Louis Brewer Hall (Gainesville, Fla., 1962); *De claris mulieribus,* trans. Guido A. Guarino (New Brunswick, N.J., 1963); *Genealogia deorum gentilium libri.*

5. *Minor Poems,* ed. MacCracken, pt. 2, no. 26. For a discussion of the career of Humphrey of Gloucester, see Vickers, *Humphrey Duke of Gloucester;* Walter F. Schirmer, *Der englische Fruhumanismus* (Tübingen, 1963), 19–50; Weiss, *Humanism in England,* 39 ff.

6. Hammond, "Poet and Patron in the *Fall of Princes,*" 121–36.

7. Hammond, "Lydgate and Coluccio Salutati," 49–57.

8. Hammond, *English Verse Between Chaucer and Surrey,* 142–45. Norton-Smith (*John Lydgate: Poems,* 114–15) argues that Lydgate finished the *Fall of Princes* before the letter was written.

9. These lines are printed in Hammond, *Chaucer to Surrey,* 197, ll. 40–44.

10. *Fall of Princes,* ed. Bergen, vol. 1, p. xlvii. For further consideration of the relation between Lydgate's and Laurent's version, see Patricia M. Gathercole, "Lydgate's *Fall of Princes* and the French Version of Boccaccio's *De Casibus,*" in *Miscellanea di Studi e Ricerche sul Quattrocento francesse,* ed. F. Simone (Turin, 1966), 167–78; Herbert G. Wright, *Boccaccio in England from Chaucer to Tennyson* (London, 1957), 5–23.

11. *Fall of Princes,* vol. 1, p. liii.

12. Ibid., 1.3844–4242; see also vol. 4, pp. 151–55.

13. Ibid., vol. 4, p. 153.

14. Ibid., vol. 4, pp. 153–54.

15. Ibid., vol. 4, pp. 154–55.

16. See also ibid., 4.3991–4004.

17. Ibid., 2.806–917.

18. John of Salisbury, *Policraticus,* ed. Murray F. Markland (New York, 1979), bks. 5–6.

19. *Fall of Princes,* 2.2234 ff., 3494 ff., 3.2206 ff., 3872 ff., 4.2332 ff.

20. Ibid., 4.638, 2640 ff., 3137 ff., 5.2341 ff., 6.750 ff.

21. Note the difference between this view and Pearsall's (*John Lydgate,* 241–42).

22. *Fall of Princes,* 2420 ff.

23. Ibid., 8.2431–57.

24. Ibid., 8.3165–3206.

25. For similar sentiments, see the prologue to *Troy Book,* ES, 97 (1906), ll. 147 ff. and Guido, *Historia,* prologue, ll. 1–14.

26. For a description of the manuscripts and prints, see *Fall of Princes,* ed. Bergen, vol. 4, pp. 3–123; Schirmer, *John Lydgate,* 225–26; Pearsall, *John Lydgate,* 250–51.

27. A. S. G. Edwards, "The Influence of Lydgate's *Fall of Princes* c. 1440–1559: A Survey," *MS* 39 (1977):424–39; and "John Lydgate, Medieval Antifeminism and Harley 2251," *AnM* 13 (1972):32–44. For other descriptions of these anthologies, see Hammond, *Chaucer to Surrey,* 155–56; *Fall of Princes,* ed. Bergen, pt. 4, pp. 105, 123; *Index of Middle English Verse,* ed. Brown and Robbins (New York, 1943), 185; and *Supplement* (New York, 1965), 133.

28. *Mirror for Magistrates,* ed. L. B. Campbell (Cambridge, 1938); *The Complaint of Henry Duke of Buckingham, including the Induction, or, Thomas Sackville's Contribution to the Mirror for Magistrates,* ed. M. Hearsey, Yale Studies in English, no. 86 (New Haven, 1936).

29. For a discussion about the link between the *Fall of Princes* and Shakespeare's history plays, see Schirmer, *John Lydgate,* 226–27, and "The Importance of the Fifteenth Century," 104 ff.

Chapter Five

1. *Issue Rolls,* Easter, 2 Henry V. Die Jovis xxj, die [sic] Junis.

2. *Cal. Norman Rolls,* D.K. 42 Report, App. 375.

3. For a concise review of this critical controversy, see *John Lydgate: Poems,* ed. Norton-Smith, 119.

4. Stanzas 1–3, for example, are influenced by Horace's "Ad Navem qua vehebatur Virgilius" (*Odes,* 1.iii).

5. See Chaucer, *Works,* ed. Robinson, V (F) 1045 ff.

6. *Minor Poems,* ed. MacCracken, pt. 2, no. 26.

7. Ibid., no. 27.

8. Schirmer, *John Lydgate,* 121.

9. Ibid., 118. For the broader historical and political context of this and related poems, see John W. McKenna, "Henry VI of England and the Dual Monarchy: Aspects of Royal Political Propaganda," *Journal of the Warburg and Courtland Institutes* 28 (1965):145–62; B. J. H. Rowe, "King Henry VI's Claim to France in Picture and Poem," *Library,* 4th ser. 13 (1933):77–88.

10. Pearsall, *John Lydgate,* 167; Schirmer, *John Lydgate,* 74.
11. Schirmer, *John Lydgate,* 94.
12. *Minor Poems,* ed. MacCracken, pt. 1, no. 64; pt. 2, no. 69.
13. See, for example, *Brut,* ed. Frederick Brie, EETS, OS, 131, 136 (London, 1906–8), 45 ff.; Gregory's *Chronicle,* Camden Society (London, 1876), 164 ff.; *Henry VI,* ed. M. E. Christie (London, 1922), 51 ff.
14. *Brut,* ed. Brie, 450 ff.
15. *Minor Poems,* ed. MacCracken, pt. 2, nos. 28–29.
16. Ibid., p. 624.
17. Ibid., no. 30.
18. Ibid., no. 32.
19. See, for example, the accounts in *The Chronicles of Enguerrand de Monstrelet,* trans. Thomas Johnes (London, 1810), 7:46 ff., and *Journal d'un bourgois de Paris sous le Regne de Francois Premier* (Paris, 1854). 248 ff.
20. For a description of Carpenter's activities, see T. Brewer, *Memorial of the Life and Times of John Carpenter* (London, 1856); Pearsall, *John Lydgate,* 171.
21. MacKenzie, *The Poems of William Dunbar,* no. 64. For a consideration of the relation of Lydgate and Dunbar, see P. H. Nichols, "William Dunbar as a Scottish Lydgatian," *PMLA* 46 (1931):214–24; Ronald D. S. Jack. "Dunbar and Lydgate," *SSL* 8 (1971):215–27.
22. *Minor Poems,* ed. MacCracken, pt. 2, no. 33; MacKenzie, *The Poems of William Dunbar,* no. 26.
23. *Minor Poems,* ed. MacCracken, pt. 2, nos. 11, 54.
24. Ibid., no. 41.
25. Ibid., no. 40.
26. Ibid., no. 43.
27. Ibid., nos. 45–46.
28. Ibid., nos. 44, 42.
29. Ibid., no. 64.

Chapter Six

1. Spurgeon, ed., *Chaucer Criticism and Allusion,* 1:70; Hawes, *Pastime of Pleasure,* ed. Mead, ll. 32–34.
2. *Minor Poems,* ed. MacCracken, pt. 2.
3. Ibid., no. 56.
4. Ibid., nos. 58–59.
5. Ibid., no. 57.
6. Chaucer, *Works,* ed. Robinson, I (A) 4134.
7. *Minor Poems,* ed. MacCracken, pt. 2, no. 66.
8. Ibid., no. 76.
9. *Poems of William Dunbar,* ed. MacKenzie, no. 9.
10. *Minor Poems,* ed. MacCracken, pt. 2, no. 70.

11. Ibid., nos. 61–62, 60, 68.

12. Ibid., nos. 65, 74.

13. Ibid., nos. 63, 73.

14. *Poems of William Dunbar,* ed. MacKenzie, no. 7. For a consideration of the relation of Lydgate's and Dunbar's poems, see R. D. S. Jack, "Dunbar and Lydgate," *SSL* 8 (1971):215–27.

15. *Minor Poems,* ed. MacCracken, pt. 2, nos. 13, 17, 12.

16. Ibid., no. 9.

17. Ibid., nos. 38, 14, 39, 18–19.

18. *Poems of William Dunbar,* ed. MacKenzie, no. 1.

19. *Minor Poems,* ed. MacCracken, pt. 2, no. 20. For an interesting discussion of the significance of the term *fabula* in the Middle Ages, see R. T. Lenaghan, "The Nun's Priest's Fable," *PMLA* 78 (1963):310 ff.; Wesley Trimpy, "The Ancient Hypothesis of Fiction: An Essay on the Origins of Literary Theory," *Traditio* 27 (1971):1–78.

20. *Minor Poems,* ed. MacCracken, pt. 2, no. 24. For a useful consideration of this issue, see Pearsall, *John Lydgate,* 192–93.

21. Robert Henryson, *Fables,* in *The Poems of Robert Henryson,* ed. Denton Fox (Oxford, 1981), 5–9.

22. *Minor Poems,* ed. MacCracken, pt. 2, nos. 20, 23, 21.

Chapter Seven

1. Pearsall, *John Lydgate,* 268; Rosemary Woolf, *The English Religious Lyric in the Middle Ages* (Oxford, 1968), 199, 281.

2. *Minor Poems,* ed. MacCracken, pt. 1, nos. 15, 49.

3. For a brief comparison of the "Ballade" and the *Anticlaudianus,* see *John Lydgate: Poems,* ed. Norton-Smith, 143–44.

4. *Minor Poems of the Vernon MS.,* pt. 1, ed. C. Horstmann, EETS, OS, 98 (London, 1892), 298.

5. *Minor Poems,* ed. MacCracken, pt. 1, nos. 5, 17–18, 69.

6. Ibid., no. 14.

7. Ibid., nos. 17, 11.

8. Ibid., no. 17.

9. For a description of this scene, see John Stow, *A Survey of London,* ed. C. L. Kingsford (Oxford, 1971), 2:230 ff.

10. *Pilgrimage of the Life of Man,* ed. Furnivall and Locock.

11. Guillaume de Deguileville, *Le pélerinage de vie humaine,* ed. J. Stürzinger (London, 1893); *Le pélerinage de l'âme,* ed. J. Stürzinger (London, 1895); *Le pélerinage Jhesu-crist,* ed. J. Stürzinger (London, 1897).

12. *Minor Poems,* ed. MacCracken, pt. 1, no. 1.

13. Ibid., nos. 3, 16.

14. Ibid., no, 7.

15. For a consideration of Lydgate's style in the lyrics, see *John Lydgate: Poems,* ed. Norton-Smith, 144–50, 192–95; Pearsall, *John Lydgate,* 270 ff.; Walter Schirmer, "Der Stil in Lydgates religose Dichtung," in *Kleine Schriften* (Tübingen, 1950), 40–56; Isabel Hyde, "Lydgate's 'Haff Chongyd Latyne': An Illustration," *MLN* 70 (1955):252–54. For a more general discussion of Lydgate's aureate style, see Elfriede Tilgner, *Die Aureate Terms als Stilelement bie Lydgate* (Berlin, 1936).

16. *Minor Poems,* ed. MacCracken, pt. 1, nos. 45, 8.

17. Ibid., no. 39.

18. Ibid., no. 21.

19. Ibid., nos. 30, 29.

20. Schirmer, *John Lydgate,* 190.

21. *Minor Poems,* ed. MacCracken, pt. 1, no. 23.

22. Ibid., nos. 26, 28, 32.

23. Schirmer, *John Lydgate,* 187–88.

24. *Minor Poems,* ed. MacCracken, pt. 1, nos. 23, 20, 31, 21.

25. Ibid., nos. 47–48, 42.

26. Ibid., nos. 46, 43.

27. This poem is printed by O. Glauning, in *Lydgate's Two Nightingale Poems,* EETS, ES, 80 (London, 1900).

28. *Minor Poems,* ed. MacCracken, pt. 1, pp. xxxiii–xxxiv. See, for example, Pearsall, *John Lydgate,* 267–68; Schirmer, *John Lydgate,* 181.

29. *Minor Poems,* ed. MacCracken, pt. 1, no. 68.

30. For a similar view, see Schirmer, *John Lydgate,* 149–51.

31. *Minor Poems,* ed. MacCracken, pt. 1, nos. 33–34.

32. Ibid., nos. 37, 36, 38.

33. Ibid., nos. 36, 38.

34. *St. Edmund and Fremund,* ed. C. Horstmann, in *Altenglische Legenden* (Heilbronn, 1881), 376–445; *The Life of Saint Alban and Saint Amphibal,* ed. J. E. Van Der Westhuizen (London, 1974).

35. Johannes Amundesham's *Annals of St. Albans,* ed. H. T. Riley, Rolls Series (London, 1870–71), 2:256, lxiii.

36. For a useful consideration of the poem's style, see *John Lydgate: Poems,* ed. Norton-Smith, 144.

37. *Minor Poems,* ed. MacCracken, pt. 1, nos. 54, 63.

38. Ibid., nos. 54, 53, 55.

39. *A Critical Edition of John Lydgate's Life of Our Lady,* ed. Joseph A. Lauritis (Pittsburgh, 1961). For a discussion of the style of this work, see also J. A. Lauritis, "Second Thoughts on Style in Lydgate's *Life of Our Lady,"* in *Essays and Studies in Language and Literature,* ed. H. E. Petit (Pittsburgh, 1964), 12–13.

Chapter Eight

1. Joseph Ritson, *Bibliographia poetica* (London, 1802), 87 ff.
2. See, for example, Spurgeon, ed., *Chaucer Criticism and Allusion,* 1:46, 49, 54, 71, 73, 77.
3. Ibid., 1:54.
4. Ibid., 1:46, 71, 68, 73, 76, 77.
5. John Metham, *Amoryus and Cleopes,* ed. Hardin Craig, EETS, OS, 132 (London, 1916), ll. 2192–95.
6. Spurgeon, ed., *Chaucer Criticism and Allusion,* 1:70.
7. Hawes, *Pastime of Pleasure,* ed. Mead, ll. 1373–93.
8. Ibid., ll. 27 ff.
9. Spurgeon, ed., *Chaucer Criticism and Allusion,* 1:14.
10. Ibid., 1:19; see also 1:24.
11. *Siege of Thebes,* ed. Erdman, ll. 53–56.
12. *Fall of Princes,* ed. Bergen, 3:3858–60.
13. Spurgeon, ed., *Chaucer Criticism and Allusion,* 1:45.
14. Hawes, *Pastime of Pleasure,* ed. Mead, ll. 1317 ff.
15. Spurgeon, ed., *Chaucer Criticism and Allusion,* 1:68, 73, 77; John Skelton, *Poetical Works,* 75, 377–79.
16. Spurgeon, ed., *Chaucer Criticism and Allusion,* 1:76.
17. Skelton, "Philip Sparrow," ll. 806–7.
18. Skelton, "Garlande of Laurell," ll. 428–34.
19. Skelton, "Philip Sparrow," ll. 805–10.

Selected Bibliography

PRIMARY SOURCES

1. Editions

Bergen, Henry. *Troy Book.* Early English Text Society, Extra Series 97, 103, 106, 126. London: Kegan Paul, Trench, Trübner & Co., 1906–20.

———. *Fall of Princes.* Early English Text Society, Extra Series 108, 125. London: Oxford University Press, 1924–27.

Erdmann, Axel, and **Ekwall, Eilert.** *Siege of Thebes.* Early English Text Society, Extra Series 108, 125. London: Oxford University Press, 1911–20.

Furnivall, F. J., and **Locock, Katherine B.** Deguileville's *Pilgrimage of the Life of Man.* Early English Text Society, Extra Series, 77, 83, 92. London: Kegan, Paul, Trench, Trübner & Co., 1899–1904.

Horstmann, Carl. *St. Edmund and Fremund.* In *Altenglische Lengenden.* Heilbronn: Henninger, 1881.

Lauritis, J. A., et al. *A Critical Edition of John Lydgate's Life of Our Lady.* Duquesne Studies, Philological Series, no. 2. Pittsburgh: Duquesne University Press, 1961.

MacCracken, Henry Noble. *The Minor Poems of John Lydgate.* Early English Text Society, Extra Series, 107, Original Series 192. London: Oxford University Press, 1911–34. (Part 1, religious poems; part 2, secular poems).

Schick, J. *The Temple of Glas.* Early English Text Society, Extra Series 60. London: Kegan Paul, Trench, Trübner & Co., 1891. A more recent text is available in *John Lydgate: Poems,* ed. Norton-Smith (see below).

Sieper, Ernst. *Resoun and Sensuallyte.* Early English Text Society, Extra Series 84, 89. London: Oxford University Press, 1901–3.

Steele, R. *Secrees of Old Philisoffres.* Early English Text Society, Extra Series 66. London: Kegan Paul, Trench, Trübner & Co., 1894.

Westhuizen, J. E. van der. *The Life of Saint Alban and Saint Amphibal.* Leiden: Brill, 1974.

2. Selections

Hammond, Eleanor P. *English Verse Between Chaucer and Surrey.* 1927. Reprint. New York: Octagon Books, 1969.

Norton-Smith, John. *John Lydgate: Poems.* Clarendon Medieval and Tudor Series. Oxford: Clarendon Press, 1966.

SECONDARY SOURCES

1. Bibliographies

Edwards, A. S. G. "A Lydgate Bibliography, 1928–68." *Bulletin of Bibliography* 27 (1970):95–98.

Renoir, Alain, and **Benson, C. David.** "John Lydgate." In *A Manual of the Writings in Middle English 1050–1500,* edited by Albert E. Hartung, 1809–1920, 2071–2175. New Haven: Connecticut Academy of Arts and Sciences, 1980.

2. Books and Articles

Atwood, E. B. "Some Minor Sources of Lydgate's *Troy Book.*" *Studies in Philology* 35 (1938):25–42. Minimizes importance of Old French sources; stresses influence of Ovid, Chaucer, and Isidore of Seville.

Ayers, R. W. "Medieval History, Moral Purpose, and the Structure of Lydgate's *Siege of Thebes.*" *Publications of the Modern Language Association* 73 (1958):463–74. Argues that the *Siege of Thebes* reflects the English political situation at the time Lydgate wrote.

Benson, C. David. *The History of Troy in Middle English Literature.* Suffolk: D. S. Brewer, 1980. Pp. 97–132. Stresses Lydgate's skill in handling the Troy matter and in developing a genuine historical perspective in his version.

Bowers, R. H. "Iconography in Lydgate's *Dance of Death.*" *Southern Folklore Quarterly* 12 (1948):111–28. Argues Lydgate's poem is part of a medieval tradition that ended in eighteenth-century graveyard poetry.

Dwyer, R. A. "Arthur's Stellification in the *Fall of Princes.*" *Philological Quarterly* 57 (1978):155–71. Considers Lydgate's independent treatment of Arthurian matter in the *Fall of Princes.*

Ebin, L. "Lydgate's Views on Poetry." *Annuale Mediaevale* 18 (1977):76–105. Argues that Lydgate develops a critical terminology to describe his activities as poet.

Edwards, A. S. G. "Lydgate's Attitudes to Women." *English Studies* 51 (1970):436–47. Challenges Renoir's views about Lydgate's representation of women.

———. "John Lydgate, Medieval Antifeminism and Harley 2251." *Annuale Medievale* 13 (1972):32–44. Prints Lydgate's antifeminist passages together with annotator's comments.

———. "The Influence of Lydgate's *Fall of Princes* c. 1440–1559: A Survey." *Mediaeval Studies* 39 (1977):424–39. Considers ways in which

Lydgate's poem was utilized in the late Middle Ages both in its entirety and in anthologies.

Farnham, W. *The Medieval Heritage of Elizabethan Tragedy.* Oxford: Basil Blackwell, 1936. Pp. 160–72. Useful on Lydgate's relation to Boccaccio and his view of tragedy.

Gathercole, P. "Lydgate's *Fall of Princes* and the French Version of Boccaccio's *De Casibus.*" In *Miscellanea di Studi e Ricerche sul Quattrocento francese,* edited by F. Simone, 167–78. Turin: Giappichelli, 1966. Provides details of Lydgate's manipulation of his immediate source.

Hascall, D. L. "The Prosody of John Lydgate." *Language and Studies* 3 (1970):122–46. An important reassessment of Lydgate's prosody in terms of the fifteenth-century poets' effort to reestablish a literary medium in English.

Hammond, E. P. "Poet and Patron in the *Fall of Princes.*" *Anglia* 38 (1914):121–36. Examines Lydgate's relation with Humphrey of Gloucester.

———. "The 9-syllabled Pentameter Line in Some Post Chaucerian Manuscripts." *Modern Philology* 23 (1925–26):129–52. Examines the use of headless and broken-backed lines in some fifteenth-century texts including Lydgate's "Complaint of the Black Knight."

———. "Lydgate and Coluccio Salutati." *Modern Philology* 25 (1927):49–57. Argues that Humphrey of Gloucester encouraged Lydgate to incorporate the story of Lucretia from Coluccio Salutati's work.

Hyde, I. "Lydgate's 'Halff Chongyd Latyne': An Illustration." *Modern Language Notes* 70 (1955):252–4. Documents correspondence between Lydgate's aureate language in his "Ballade" and the *Anticlaudianus.*

Jack, R. D. S. "Dunbar and Lydgate." *Studies in Scottish Literature* 8 (1971):215–27. Discusses Lydgate's influence on Dunbar's poems.

Lampe, D. "Lydgate's Laughter: 'Horse, Goose, and Sheep' as Social Satire." *Annuale Mediaevale* 15 (1974):150–58. Stresses the originality of Lydgate's treatment in this poem.

Lewis, C. S. "The Fifteenth Century Heroic Line." *Essays and Studies* 24 (1938):28–41. Offers a general theory of fifteenth-century metrics.

Lauritis, J. A. "Second Thoughts on Style in Lydgate's *Life of Our Lady.*" In *Essays and Studies in Language and Literature,* edited by H. E. Petit, 12–23. Duquesne Studies, Philological Series, no. 5. Pittsburgh: Duquesne University Press, 1964. Enumerates the "bardic" traits recognizable in Lydgate's style in this poem.

McKenna, J. W. "Henry VI of England and the Dual Monarchy: Aspects of Royal Political Propaganda, 1422–32." *Journal of the Warburg and Courtauld Institute* 28 (1965):145–62. Considers the theme of the dual monarchy in Lydgate's poems.

Manzalaoui, M. A. "Lydgate and English Prosody." In *Cairo Studies in English,* edited by M. Wahba, 87–104. Cairo, 1960. Reconciles theories of Schick and Lewis.

Marquard, W. F. "A Source for the Passage on the Origin of Chess in Lydgate's *Troy Book." Modern Language Notes* 64 (1949):87–88. Links this passage with Jacobus de Cessolis *De Ludo Saccorum.*

Miskimin, A. "Patterns in *The Kingis Quair* and the *Temple of Glas." Papers on Language and Literature* 13 (1972):339–61. Defines Lydgate's influence on the design of the *Kingis Quair.*

Miller, J. I., Jr. "Lydgate the Hagiographer as Literary Artist." In *The Learned and the Lewed: Studies in Chaucer and Medieval Literature,* edited by Larry D. Benson, 279–90. Cambridge: Harvard University Press, 1979. Stresses Lydgate's independence and skill in his saints' lives.

Nichols, P. H. "Dunbar as a Scottish Lydgatian." *Publications of the Modern Language Society* 46 (1931):214–24. Reveals the influence of Lydgate on Dunbar's Marian poetry.

———. "Lydgate's Influence on the Aureate Terms of the Scottish Chaucerians." *Publications of the Modern Language Society* 47 (1932):516–22. Suggests direct influence of Lydgate's aureate language on the Middle Scots poets.

Norton-Smith, J. "Lydgate's Changes in the *Temple of Glas." Medium Aevum* 27 (1958):166–72. Argues Lydgate made deliberate revisions in the poem in three different versions.

———. "Lydgate's Metaphors." *English Studies* 42 (1961):90–93. Response to Renoir's suggestions about Lydgate's metaphor of the binding knot.

Parr, J. "Astronomical Dating for Some of Lydgate's Poems." *Publications of the Modern Language Association* 67 (1952):251–58. Revises earlier views on the dating of Lydgate's poems.

Parry, P. H. "On the Continuity of English Civic Pageantry: A Study of John Lydgate and the Tudor Pageant." *Forum for Modern Language Studies* 15 (1979):222–36. Argues that English civic pageantry changed little between 1400 and 1600.

Pearsall, D. *John Lydgate.* London: Routledge & Kegan Paul, 1970. The most important critical study of the entire corpus of Lydgate's poems.

———. "The English Chaucerians." In *Chaucer and Chaucerians,* edited by D. S. Brewer, 203–22. London: Nelson, 1966. Useful on the relation of Chaucer's and Lydgate's style, language, and versification.

Pyle, F. "The Pedigree of Lydgate's Heroic Line." *Hermathena* 50 (1937):26–59. Traces the history of Lydgate's line back to the *Poema Morale.*

Renoir, A. "The Binding Knot: Three Uses of One Image in Lydgate's Poetry." *Neophilologus* 41 (1957):202–4. Considers Lydgate's skillful use of this metaphor in the *Temple of Glas,* "Mumming at Hertford," and "A Gentlewoman's Lament."

———. "Attitudes Towards Women in Lydgate's *Siege of Thebes.*" *English Studies* 42 (1961):1–14. Surveys Lydgate's representation of women and argues that his response is extremely varied.

———. "The Immediate Source of Lydgate's *Siege of Thebes.*" *Studia Neophilologica* 33 (1961):86–95. Argues Lydgate's source is a complete text of the *Roman de Edipus.*

———. *The Poetry of John Lydgate.* Cambridge, Mass.: Harvard University Press, 1967. Considers Lydgate in his major poems as a poet who anticipates the Renaissance.

Schibanoff, S. "Avarice and Cerberus in Coluccio Salutati's *De Laboribus Herculis* and Lydgate's *Fall of Princes.*" *Modern Philology* 71 (1973–74):390–92. Stresses Lydgate's borrowing from Salutati in his unconventional treatment of avarice.

Schirmer, W. F. *John Lydgate: A Study in the Culture of the XVth Century.* Translated by Ann E. Keep, Berkeley and Los Angeles: University of California Press, 1961. Originally published in German in 1952. A useful study of Lydgate's work in the context of the historical and political events of his time.

———. "Der Stil in Lydgates religiose Dichtung," In *Kleine Schriften,* 40–56. Tübingen: Max Niemeyer, 1950. A study of the stylistic features of Lydgate's religious verse.

Schlauch, M. "Stylistic Attributes of John Lydgate's Prose." In *To Honor Roman Jakobson,* 3:1757–68. The Hague: Mouton, 1967. Discusses specific practices in Lydgate's prose and larger questions of style.

Studer, J. "History as Moral Instruction: John Lydgate's Record of *Troie Toun.*" *Emporia State Research Studies* 19, no. 1 (1970):5–13, 22. Argues Lydgate moralized the story of Troy.

Tilgner, E. *Die Aureate Terms als Stilelement bei Lydgate.* Berlin: Paul Funk, 1936. A detailed analysis of Lydgate's aureate language.

Wilson, J. "Poet and Patron in Early Fifteenth Century England: John Lydgate's *Temple of Glas.*" *Parergon* 11 (1975):25–32. On the possibilities of the Paston patronage for the *Temple of Glas.*

Wright, H. G. *Boccaccio in England from Chaucer to Tennyson.* London: Athlone Press, 1957. Pp. 5–23. Considers Lydgate's sources in Boccaccio in terms of theme, attitude, and style.

Index

DATE DUE

GAYLORD			PRINTED IN U.S.A.